D0669067

GREEK MYTHOLOGY

THESEUS - PERSEUS

Stephanides Brothers'

GREEK MYTHOLOGY

THESEUS - PERSEUS

☙

Retold by Menelaos Stephanides
Drawings by Yannis Stephanides

Translation
Bruce Walter

SIGMA

THESEUS - PERSEUS

First edition 2000, 4th run 2009
Printed in Greece by "Fotolio & Typicon", bound by G. Betsoris
© 2009 Dimitris M. Stefanidis
All rights reserved throughout the world

SIGMA PUBLICATIONS
30, Lekanidi Street, Ag. Dimitrios, 173 43 Athens, Greece
Tel.: +30 210 3607667, Fax: +30 210 3638941
www.sigmabooks.gr, e-mail: sbooks@sigmabooks.gr

ISBN-10: 960-425-075-2
ISBN-13: 978-960-425-075-2

HEROES: men mighty, unflinching and fair in spirit, mind and body. They may not have been quite as men envisaged them in those distant, mythical years, yet they did exist. For there have always been heroes and always will be. As long as there is cowardice, there will be daring, as long as there is evil, there will be virtue, too; as long as there is meanness of spirit, there will be generosity. For the bad gives birth to the good as the winter brings the spring. The common man loves a hero. He places his trust in him and draws strength from his example – that strength which has enabled mankind to forge onwards and upwards.

CONTENTS

PERSEUS

The forebears of Perseus

Like all the greatest heroes of Greek myths, Perseus could trace his ancestry back to the very beginnings of time. In fact, his line first sprang from Chaos and Mother Earth, whose best-known children were the Titans. The most renowned of these, Oceanus, was the father of all the rivers of the world and his son, the river-god Inachus, became the first to rule in Argos and the founder of a line that numbered not only Perseus but even Heracles among its ranks.

While Inachus built Argos, and Perseus became that city's mightiest hero, many of the generations that were born between these two lived far away from Greece. How that came about is recounted in the myth of Io, Inachus' unlucky daughter, who was loved by Zeus but hounded from her home by the jealous fury of his wife Hera. Mercilessly hunted down, Io finally reached the banks of the Nile and there gave birth to Epaphus, who was destined to become the first of all the kings of Egypt.

How the descendants of the unhappy Io eventually re-established themselves in the city of their forebears is the subject of this tragic story.

Epaphus had a daughter, Libya, who married the sea god Poseidon and had a son by him named Belus. He, too, ruled the territory watered by the Nile and being a powerful sovereign he overthrew the neighbouring monarchs to the east and west, renaming the latter's territory Libya in honour of his mother. Having done so, he installed his own sons in their place: Aegyptus as ruler of Arabia and Danaus in the kingdom to the west.

These two brothers, parted from their youth and ruling over widely separated kingdoms, had nothing in common save that each of them eventually fathered fifty children. However, those of Aegyptus were all boys, while Danaus had only girls; and this, of course, made Aegyptus much the stronger of the two.

When Belus died, Aegyptus moved in swiftly with his army, and with the help of his fifty sons he conquered the land of the Nile, which has borne the name of Egypt ever since. Not only did he ignore the fact that Danaus, too, had rightful claims upon his father's throne, but he even launched a military campaign to seize his brother's kingdom from him.

Luckily, Danaus was given warning by the goddess Athena, who advised him to take his fifty daughters and flee to Argos, the land of his ancestors Inachus and Io.

Danaus took the goddess's advice and decided to leave for Greece. How could he stand up to Aegyptus and his fifty sons, when all he had was daughters?

It was fortunate for them all that he had given the girls a hard upbringing and made them used to working with their hands. And so, with their help, he built a ship for fifty rowers, the largest the world had ever seen. The task completed, he placed his daughters at the oars and they all set off for distant Argos, leaving their beloved Libya behind forever.

For days on end their ship hauled northwards over the waves; and when at last they did sight land it proved to be not Argos but the island of Rhodes. Yet at least it was a place to shelter and seek rest. Danaus and his daughters went ashore, and, to thank the goddess for saving them, he put up a statue to her which came to be known as the Athena of Lindos. Then he asked the gods to grant his family a safe and speedy voyage to Argos.

The next morning they set off once again. Zeus himself kept watch over their ship, and so it was that a few days later, tired but happy, they reached the land of their ancestors.

At this time Argos was ruled by a king named Gelanor, and Danaus sought his protection; for he feared that the sons of Aegyptus would not be content to let him flee, but would pursue him wherever he went.

Gelanor looked doubtful. Then the daughters of Danaus, the Danaids as they were called, fell on their knees and begged him in the name of Zeus and of their common forebears, Io and Inachus, to show some feeling for their plight and grant them refuge.

The king still hesitated. If he helped Danaus, this would mean war with all-powerful Aegyptus – and no greater misfortune could possibly fall upon Argos. If, on the other hand, he did not give shelter to his guests he would be breaking the sacred rules of hospitality laid down by Zeus himself. What was he to do?

Meanwhile, the people of the city had taken pity on Danaus and his daughters and had made up their minds to help them. After all, these voyagers were no mere strangers, but their own kind. Were they not descendants of Io, the fair daughter of Inachus? They were determined never to let the Danaids suffer the fate of that poor girl who had been pursued the wide world over by the vengeful wrath of Hera.

No sooner had they taken this decision than an event occurred which proved a stroke of fortune for Danaus and his daughters. A wolf fell on the finest and most powerful bull in all Gelanor's herds and tore it limb from limb. The people of Argos were convinced this was an omen from the gods: the wolf was the newcomer, Danaus, and the bull none other than their king. When Gelanor heard of this killing and the meaning his people had read into it, he was terrified that the omen might prove true and, like the bull, he too would lose his life. Abandoning his throne he fled the city – and Danaus was proclaimed king of Argos in his place.

However, the new ruler had not even had time to rejoice in this lucky turn in his fortunes when the fifty sons of Aegyptus descended on the city.

With their coming, the whole population rose at Danaus' side. The finest warriors of Argos drew up in line for battle, and in the front rank stood the fifty Danaids. When they saw how bravely the people of the city had come to their aid they could not sit idly by. Besides, they were no milk and water creatures. Their father had taught them to use sword and spear like true warriors; and now, a second race of Amazons, they took their places in the line, ready for whatever might befall.

When the fifty sons of Aegyptus drew near and saw the fifty Danaids, lovely as goddesses and determined to defend themselves to the last, they looked at one another in astonishment. Instead of attacking, they began to discuss the possibility of some other approach; and after a while they asked Danaus if he would prefer that they settle their differences peacefully. Rather than fight his daughters, they suggested, why should they not marry them?

"But if you do not accept," they added, "we shall burn Argos to the ground!"

Danaus did not know where to turn. On the one hand he wanted at all costs to avoid a battle which might indeed mean the destruction of the city which had so willingly given him shelter; but on the other hand his hatred for the sons of Aegyptus still burned fiercely, too, and he suspected that cunning alone had been behind their offer. And so, while he finally accepted their terms, he did so only since he had no choice, and in his mind he had already plotted their downfall: while the preparations for the marriages were going forward, he secretly gave each of his daughters a dagger, ordering them to kill their husbands on the wedding night, when they lay down unsuspecting at their sides.

"And woe betide you if you disobey," he added. "The gods have laid down harsh penalties for disobedience of such kind."

The great wedding was celebrated with all the splendour that the sons of Aegyptus could have desired. Little did they guess what evil fate awaited them. When the ceremonies were over and night had fallen, each couple withdrew to their chamber, where the sons of Aegyptus met their deaths one by one upon the bridal couch.

Lynceus and Hypermnestra

In one of the rooms, however, Lynceus, the most handsome of them all, was in no hurry to lie down at his young bride's side. And when the lovely Danaid Hypermnestra called him to her, furtively searching for the knife beneath her pillow, he said:

"We have done you all a great wrong. I cannot agree with my brothers. It is not right for two people to be married by force of arms. I could never thrust myself upon a woman who did not choose me of her own free will, how-

...Lynceus, the most handsome of them all, was in no hurry to lie down at his young bride's side...

ever much her beauty had bewitched me."

And with these words he took a blanket, stretched himself down in the far corner of the room and was soon overcome by sleep.

Meanwhile, Hypermnestra could not even close her eyes. The young man's unexpected words had banished the hatred she once felt for him, and love now blossomed in her heart. And so she spent the whole night on watch behind the door, for fear that her sisters might find Lynceus alive and kill him, too.

But they, having carried out their deed, were deep in sleep, serene in the knowledge that they had done their duty, obeyed their father's orders and killed their enemies. Just before dawn broke, Hypermnestra woke Lynceus, told him what had happened in the night, and helped him to flee secretly from the palace to a place where he would be safe.

In the morning, when her father learned she had not killed her husband, his wrath was terrible. He immediately ordered her bound in chains and thrown into a cell. That very same day Hypermnestra was brought before the court, where he demanded that the death sentence be passed upon her.

Everybody present was against the girl: her father, her sisters, the judges, the spectators – and all of Argos, too. Her crime was far more serious than it seems to us today – in ignoring her father's orders she had defied laws which had been upheld since the beginning of time and her guilt was double, for she had broken faith with her sisters as well.

But at the very moment when Hypermnestra seemed certain to be condemned to death, who should appear before the court but Aphrodite, the great goddess of love.

"What are you doing?" she cried. "Yes, children should obey their parents, but there is a power greater still: the universal power of love! Think of the first couple the world ever knew, great Uranus, the sky, and lovely Gaea, goddess of the earth. Think of the example which they set for us. Gaea longs for love, and the sky floods her with it in the form of fruitful rain. The earth then brings forth seeds and nourishes the plants and animals, without which none of you could live. Think carefully, all of you! You, who condemn a girl to death because she loved, would not have come into this world but for such love. Without love, all that is beautiful in the world would be lost."

The goddess said no more, but she had not spoken in vain. While just a few moments before all had agreed that Hypermnestra should be sentenced to death, not a single voice could now be heard to blame her for her deed. Even her father was silent. Hypermnestra was declared innocent.

Freed from her chains, the lovely Danaid ran up to the acropolis of Argos, and from this vantage point she scanned the surrounding countryside for a signal from her beloved. It was not long in coming. From a nearby hilltop a beacon burst into flame to prove that Lynceus was there and safe.

Soon, all the city rejoiced in the triumph of their love, and later, when Danaus died, Lynceus became king of Argos, founding the generation that first brought Perseus into the world and later Heracles himself.

As for the other Danaids, Zeus ordered Athena and Hermes to wash away their guilt. And then, to find new husbands for them, Danaus held chariot races and invited the boldest young men in all the land of Greece to compete for his lovely daughters. One by one each victor carried away a Danaid until they were all married off. But because there were so many of them, and because each bore so many children, the tribe of the Danaids became so numerous that in the end the name Danaus was given to every inhabitant of Greece.

Now the Danaids may have been pardoned by gods and men alike, but they were never forgiven by the harsh judges of Hades. After their deaths, they were condemned to a weary and endless task: to pour water into a huge bottomless urn. Never ceasing for a moment, they carry pitchers to it – but the water flows away below, and the urn can never be filled. And so, for countless centuries, the Danaids have been punished in the underworld, paying for the hideous crime which they committed out of blind obedience to their father; and the urn which never fills has become known as "the urn of the Danaids", an eternal symbol of a hopeless task.

Acrisius and Proetus

Lynceus was succeeded on the throne of Argos by his son Abas, who in his turn fathered twin sons, Proetus and Acrisius.

We saw earlier how Aegyptus' greed made deadly enemies of him and Danaus. For all the terrible consequences of that enmity, it is not they who are remembered as the worst example of brotherly hatred, but Proetus and Acrisius. From their earliest childhood, these two boys made a name for themselves throughout Greece for their endless quarrels. So bitterly did they disagree that centuries afterwards mothers would still call out when they saw their children squabbling:

"To listen to you two, anyone would take you for Proetus and Acrisius!"

Believe it or not, many people even said that they had their first set-to when they were still inside their mother's womb! They had the poor woman in agony, and all their quarrel, it seems, was over who would come out first – for the firstborn would someday succeed to his father's throne.

As the children grew, things got even worse between them, much to the sorrow of their aged parents. At last the time came when Abas knew that he was dying, and to remove all cause of further quarrels between his sons he called them to his side and said:

"It is my desire and will that each of you should rule

over my kingdom in turn, a year at a time..."

But he died before he could say which of them should be first to take the throne, and another terrible quarrel broke out before his body was even cold in its grave.

In the end, Acrisius seized the kingdom by force, and Proetus was forced to flee to distant Lycia whose king, Iobates, not only offered him shelter but the hand of his daughter Stheneboea in marriage. It was not long before he even gave Proetus support in his claims upon the throne of Argos. With the army Iobates had provided, the young man returned home and demanded his father's kingdom from his brother. Acrisius refused, and a bloody battle was fought outside the walls of Argos. Neither brother gained the victory, however, and in the end they reluctantly agreed that Proetus should take neighbouring Tiryns while Acrisius would keep Argos.

Perseus, son of Zeus and Danae

Acrisius married Aganippe and by her had a daughter, the lovely Danae. But what he wanted even more was a son to succeed him on the throne; and so, anxious to learn if he would ever be blessed with one, he went to the oracle at Delphi.

Apollo's answer was as follows:

"Hear my words, Acrisius, son of Abas! Though you will never beget a son to hand your kingdom down to, in his place there will rule a mighty hero to whom your daughter shall give birth. But know this: it is written by the Fates that this grandson of yours shall kill you."

When Acrisius heard the answer he was terrified. Only one thought now possessed him – how to escape his destiny. To do so, he would stop at nothing. His only problem was, how could he make sure that he would never have a grandson?

Driven by fear, he built an underground prison with heavy bronze doors and there he shut up his daughter, Danae. To him, this seemed the perfect way of making sure she would not marry and thus never bear a child.

But Danae was so beautiful that Zeus himself had fallen in love with her, and no jail, however strong, was proof against the desires of the ruler of gods and men.

And so Zeus entered Danae's dark prison, slipping through the chinks in the shuttered window in a shower of

...Zeus entered Danae's dark prison, slipping through the chinks in the shuttered window in a shower of golden rain...

golden rain; and nine months afterwards the daughter of Acrisius gave birth to Perseus, son of Zeus.

A few days later, Acrisius was passing his daughter's cell when he heard a baby crying. Although he was sure his ears were playing tricks on him, he opened the bronze door and stood rooted to the spot with astonishment when he saw Danae clasping a baby to her breast.

Frightened out of his wits, and unable to imagine for an instant that this infant might be the son of Zeus, his suspicions immediately fell – where else? – upon his hated brother, Proetus. This suspicion soon hardened into certainty, and with it his hatred for his brother swelled. To be revenged upon him, and at the same time rid himself of this mortally dangerous grandson, he decided to kill both his daughter and her child. But at the last moment, his nerve failed him and he held back. In the end, however, a cunning plan came into his mind, and his eyes gleamed craftily as he said:

"Let the foaming waves swallow them up; let the fishes eat them. It will be Proetus' loss, not mine. If he couldn't kill me all these years, I won't let myself sit and be killed now by his son!"

And without further delay, he ordered his plan to be carried out.

A short time after this, on Seriphos, an island which lies across the gulf from Argos, a fisherman named Dictys was pulling in his nets when he saw that a wooden chest was caught up in them. Seized with curiosity, he dragged on the ropes with all his might, and soon the chest was lying on the sand. It was a fine piece of workmanship, sturdily bound in bronze. The more Dictys looked at it, the more curious he became. Where had it come from, and what could be inside?

He tried to open it, but this was no easy task. The chest was firmly sealed. Dictys was a patient man, however, and one by one he prised off the copper binding strips till in the end the lid was freed and the trunk came open. And then, to his astonishment, he saw two human forms, weak and battered by the waves, but still alive – a young woman and her baby. They were Danae and Perseus, of course. Acrisius had shut them in the chest and thrown them into the sea to meet their fate.

Dictys revived the pair and took them to his house. He

gave Danae a room of her own and provided her with all she needed to bring her young child up.

Now the king of the island, Polydectes, was Dictys' brother – a man as hard and pitiless as the fisherman was kind. He hated all women, and had sworn that he would never marry. But as soon as he set eyes on Danae, he was so blinded by her beauty that he wished to take her for his wife. And when Danae refused, he not only persisted in his attentions but began to threaten her, too. All this had quite the opposite effect to what he had intended, and the young mother felt nothing but hatred towards the king.

Perseus cuts off the fearsome Medusa's head

The years rolled by, and Perseus grew up into a strongly-built young man whom none could match in good looks, intelligence and strength. Polydectes, in the meantime, had never ceased pressing Danae to marry him, but now he had to reckon not only with her own reluctance but the opposition of young Perseus, who defended his mother fearlessly.

In the end, Polydectes decided that Perseus was a thorn

in his side that must be removed. As he saw it, this would not only leave Danae without a protector, but the loss of her son's companionship would grieve her so much that she would no longer have the strength of will to resist the king's advances. And so he set a cunning plan in motion. He called to his palace all the leading citizens of the island, Perseus among them, and announced:

"I have decided after all not to marry Danae, but to seek the hand of Hippodameia, daughter of king Oenomaus of Pissa. However, since I am but king of a small island, and do not wish to cut a poor figure before the king of mighty Pissa, it seems to me that my best chance of impressing him is by going with rich gifts. For this reason, I would like each one of you to let me have a horse to offer Oenomaus."

They all assented save Perseus, who replied sadly:

"I have neither a horse nor the money to buy one. Order me to bring you whatever else you wish, however. I am so pleased that you no longer wish to marry my mother that I will even bring you the head of the Medusa if that is your desire."

Now everyone knew that the Medusa was a fearsome

gorgon whose head had the power to turn all those that set eyes on it to stone. This meant, of course, that no one could cut it off. The phrase Perseus had used was common enough and merely showed his willingness to be of service, but as soon as Polydectes heard it, he seized his opportunity and shouted:

"Bravo! Just the gift I wanted! Go and bring me the gorgon's head and you may rest assured that I will never trouble your mother again."

Perseus was startled by this unexpected reply, but not shaken. Looking at Polydectes with cold anger, he told him:

"You shall have the head. I am leaving this instant." And with these words he marched boldly out of the hall, while Polydectes turned to his friends with a sneer on his lips and said:

"I no longer need your horses. Everything has gone according to plan. Perseus has been sent exactly where I intended. Now that Danae is alone, I am sure to make her my wife."

Indeed, the task Perseus had set himself was not only impossible but meant certain death. For as soon as he set eyes on the fearsome gorgon, he would be turned into a lifeless statue.

The Medusa lived with her two sisters on an island in the great ocean, at the very edge of the world. All three were hideous monsters with great black wings and scaly bodies. Their fingers ended in cruel talons, and instead of hair their heads were covered by a writhing mass of venomous snakes. Their tongues and two great fangs stuck out from their mouths and their whole appearance was so hideous that whoever looked on them was turned at once to stone. How could anyone cut the head off one of these vile monsters, and how could Polydectes not gloat in triumph at sending Perseus on a fatal mission?

But Perseus was the son of Zeus, ruler of gods and men – and Zeus would never let a child of his meet such a fate. Instead, he ordered Hermes and Athena to come to the young man's aid. Hermes gave Perseus a sword which could sever the Medusa's head with a single blow. It was made of solid diamond, and was so keen that it could cleave the hardest steel. The goddess Athena gave him a shield so brightly polished it made a splendid mirror.

"Since you cannot look in the Medusa's face," she told

him, "you must follow its reflection in the shield to cut her head off."

Next Athena bore Perseus away to the island of Samos, where there were life-sized images of all three gorgons.

"This one is the Medusa," said the goddess, pointing her out. "I tell you this lest you should make a mistake and try to kill one of the other two – for her sisters are immortal, and you will not only fail to harm them but lose your life in the attempt. Yet even when you try to sever the Medusa's head you will be in no small danger, unless you are properly equipped. For this reason you must go and find the three Stygian nymphs, who will give you the other things you need to carry out your mission. Where you can find them, however, nor I nor any mortal knows, only the three Graeae, hideous old crones who live near the land of the Hesperides. But they are the sisters of the Medusa, and will not tell you where the nymphs can be found unless you bend them to your will." Finally, Athena put Perseus on the road he must follow to find the Graeae, adding that he would recognise them because they had but one eye and one tooth in all, which they shared among the three of them.

Encouraged by the goddess's help, Perseus set off in search of the Graeae.

After a seemingly endless journey he found them – and just at the moment when one of them had taken out the eye to give it to her sister. For that brief instant, not one of them could see a thing – and Perseus seized his opportunity. Placing his palm beneath her outstretched fist, he let her drop the eye into his hand! Closing his fingers around it he shouted:

"There goes your eye – and you will not get it back until you tell me where to find the Stygian nymphs!"

This was an unexpected blow for the Graeae. Panic-stricken and confused, they groped blindly around in the hope of catching Perseus. They had not the slightest wish to tell him where the nymphs might be found, for in their keeping were the winged sandals, the helmet of Hades and the magic wallet Perseus needed for his task. All three Graeae could see into the future, and they knew that whoever acquired these objects would be able to kill their sister, the Medusa.

When they saw their eye was not to be retrieved by force, the sisters next began to beg for it, but Perseus replied:

"Tell me where I can find the Stygian nymphs, or I will fling your eye into the ocean."

"No, that would be the end for us!" the Graeae wailed in a terrified chorus. "Take pity on us poor creatures and give us back our eye. Do that, and we will help you in any way you want. Only, don't ask us to tell you where to find the nymphs."

"That is all the help I wish for – that and no other," was Perseus' reply. "Tell me, or you will never have your eye again."

The three Graeae held a muttered conference, but they could not make up their minds. Again they began to beg him for their eye.

"Tell me what I want this very instant," Perseus now threatened, "or I'll grind the thing to pulp beneath my heel!"

So appalled at this dire prospect were the three sisters that they volunteered the information as if in one voice and told him exactly where to find the Stygian nymphs.

"That's more like it!" cried Perseus. "Now, take your eye – and goodbye to you."

He soon found the three nymphs, and when he told them of his mission, they gladly handed over the winged sandals which would enable Perseus to fly through the heavens, the helmet of Hades which would render him invisible when worn, and the magic wallet which could expand to hold whatever was placed inside it.

"This is to put the gorgon's head in," they told him, "for even when severed from its body, its gaze can still turn those who look on it to stone."

And with these words they bade Perseus farewell and good fortune.

The young man took his precious gifts and soared upwards. His winged sandals bore him smoothly and swiftly through the sky, and it was not long before he reached the island of the gorgons. Then he put on his helmet and became invisible. From on high, he could make out the three vile creatures. Clustered thickly around them, and scattered all over the island stood stone images of men, worn and pitted by rain and time. Perseus now fixed his eyes on the reflection in the shield, which showed him that all three sisters were asleep. He swooped down closer and immediately picked out the Medusa. In this difficult moment Athena was by his side to lend him courage, and guide his hand if need be. Perseus looked carefully in the mirror, judged the distance to an inch and with a slashing sword-blow struck the hideous head right off. As he did so, from the gaping wound where the Gorgon's head had stood there sprang first a winged horse, Pegasus, and next a giant, Chrysaor, both fathered on the Medusa by Poseidon and destined by the fates to come into the world only when a hero had beheaded her.

Perseus immediately stuffed the bloody head into his magic wallet and soared into the air, while the corpse of the gorgon writhed like a wounded snake then slowly toppled from the rocks to the sea below. But the splash of its fall awakened her two sisters. Realising that the Medusa was dead, they immediately began a search for her slayer, first on land, then, opening their great wings, in the air above. But Perseus was absolutely invisible, and the two gorgons returned to earth in empty-handed disappointment.

Perseus flew on uneventfully until he came to a place where an astonishing spectacle met his eyes. A huge giant was holding up the heavens on his shoulders! This was Atlas, the Titan who had been condemned by mighty Zeus to bear his crushing burden for all eternity, because he had

...Perseus looked carefully in the mirror, and with a slash-ing sword-blow struck the hideous head right off...

fought against the gods in that earth-shaking conflict known as The Battle of the Titans.

Filled with wonder at Atlas' incredible strength, Perseus glided down to earth and walked up to his feet. He wanted to meet the mightiest being in the world in person. The Titan, however, did not give him a warm welcome, for it had been prophesied that a son of Zeus would come to these parts one day and steal the golden apples from the nearby Garden of the Hesperides. Although this garden was guarded by a fearsome dragon named Ladon, Atlas was still very worried about the safety of the apples.

So, when he set eyes on Perseus he stiffened in suspicion and demanded who he was and what business he had in this distant part of the world where no mortal had ever before set foot.

"I am Perseus, son of Zeus, and I have come from..."

But Atlas cut him short. As soon as he heard the words 'son of Zeus' his thoughts flew to the golden apples and he roared:

"Thief! You have come to steal our dearest treasure! Get out of my sight before I call for Ladon to tear you into pieces!"

...Seeing the Medusa's head, Atlas was turned to stone!...

"I am no thief," replied Perseus, "and I have not come to take anything away from you. I was passing this way because I have been to kill the gorgon Medusa. Here! Her head is in this sack."

"Not only a thief, but a liar," retorted Atlas. "The Medusa's head in a sack, indeed. As if it could ever be cut off!"

"But I did," said the hero. "Look!" And with these words he pulled out the hideous head and showed it to the Titan. The moment he did so, an awesome change took place before his eyes. Seeing the gorgon's head, Atlas was turned to stone! His body became a towering mountain, his hair and beard were transformed into forests, and his head was now the mountain's highest peak. And upon that peak the great arch of the sky has rested ever since. To this very day the mountain is called Atlas.

Perseus, too, was almost petrified when he realized what had happened. He had never imagined that the lifeless head would have the power to turn to stone a being as mighty as the Titan, especially since Atlas was immortal. Sad at heart, he put the head back in the wallet and flew off once again.

At this point, one might ask: but if Perseus changed Atlas

into a mountain, how is it that Heracles met him later, still bearing the world upon his shoulders? However, we must remember that mythology was not all the work of one man, and neither did it all originate in a single time or place. The myths of the Greeks are full of contradictions, and perhaps among the most striking is this one involving Atlas. Yet it should not trouble us any more than it troubled the ancients, who had no wish to spoil the wonder of a tale for the sake of mere logic!

Perseus saves Andromeda

Continuing on his way, our hero eventually reached the shores of Ethiopia. From his vantage point in the sky, he suddenly caught sight of a white speck against the dark rocks of the shore. Curious, he swooped down lower.

"What a splendid statue!" he cried out in delight as he drew nearer. "I wonder what great sculptor created this?"

But when he came closer still, he saw the wind ruffling the hair of the "statue" which, of course, was no figure of stone but a living maiden, chained to the rock and sobbing bitterly.

Perseus came to earth and approached the girl. He asked her name and why she had been left there. In a voice still torn by sobs the unhappy young woman told him her tragic story.

"My name is Andromeda," she said, "and I am the daughter of king Cepheus, who rules this land. Alas! They have tied me to this rock because I must pay for a crime which was not of my doing. My mother Cassiopeia is to blame. She dared to compare her own beauty with that of the lovely Nereids, daughters of old Nereus. She even made a quarrel of it, insisting she was fairer still than they. The sea nymphs were so insulted that they took their complaint not to their father, who never loses his temper, but to the mighty god of all the seas, earth-shaker Poseidon. When he heard them, his anger knew no bounds. To punish us, he loosed a disastrous flood upon our land, and as soon as that had receded, he sent a sea-monster which ravaged what was left of our country. Our people were in despair. And because there seemed to be no end to our troubles, my father consulted the oracle to learn what he must do. There he learned that the evils which had fallen on our land would cease only when the sea-monster had devoured the daughter of the king. For my mother, this was the worst punishment of all, for she loves me more than life itself. But though my parents could never have been persuaded to sacrifice me to the monster of their own free will, the people could bear their sufferings no longer. They rose against my father and forced him to hand me over. Then they bound me to this rock, and here, alas, I wait for the monster to tear me apart."

By the time Andromeda had finished, Perseus was close to tears. He had already fallen in love with the beautiful maiden and wanted nothing more than to rescue her and make her his wife. He was wondering how to begin to tell her this when she spoke again.

"Save me, stranger – and if you wish, make me your slave. If you do not want me for your own, then just save me, and I will be grateful to you forever. But what am I saying? I am asking for something I cannot allow to happen. For if you take me from here, the monster will go on ravaging our country." And with these words she began to sob again, weeping bitter tears at her fate.

"Do not cry, unhappy maiden," said the hero. "I am Perseus, son of Zeus and I can kill the monster first, before

I set you free."

The girl's face lit up with hope – and not only the girl's; for at this moment her parents arrived, and hearing Perseus' words they threw themselves at his feet.

"Save our daughter, stranger," they begged, "and ask what you will of us in return. Take everything we have – demand our whole kingdom and we shall gladly give it to you."

"I want none of these things," was the hero's reply. "My only wish is to have Andromeda as my wife."

And then, in their joy, Cepheus and Cassiopeia swore to Aphrodite that they would give their daughter to Perseus if he slew the fearsome monster.

At that very moment the sea began to boil. A long, black hump heaved itself out of the foam, sank back beneath the surface then reared up again, till soon the whole great length of the hideous sea-dragon could be seen above the waves. When Andromeda set eyes upon it, she let out a piercing cry, while Cepheus and Cassiopeia threw themselves terror-stricken into each other's arms. There was not a moment to lose. The monster was coming closer by the second, leaving a long furrow in its wake. Followed by the

...The huge creature thrashed and writhed, raising waves as high as mountains...

bewildered eyes of Andromeda and her parents, Perseus soared into the heavens. Clamping the helmet of Hades upon his head he immediately became invisible, to the even greater astonishment of the watchers below. Then the hero dived unseen on the monster and thrust his diamond-bladed sword into its neck; but so thick and tough was the monster's hide that the wound did no more than lash it into a frenzy. The huge creature thrashed and writhed, raising waves as high as mountains and preventing Perseus from getting in another blow. The sea-dragon searched frenziedly for its attacker, but there was nothing to be seen in sea or sky. Suddenly, however, it caught sight of Perseus' shadow on the foaming waves. Deceived, it made a vicious lunge towards it. This was the chance the hero had been waiting for, and he plunged his sword-hilt deep into the monster's head. And then, as if by magic, the beast uncoiled, rolled belly-upwards on the surface of the sea and lay there bobbing in the waves. Landing on its scaly corpse, Perseus removed his helmet and revealed himself. When Andromeda and her parents saw him standing there, they wept for joy. Once he was sure the monster was stone-dead, he flew over to Andromeda, quickly loosed her chains, gathered her gently in his arms and set her on dry land before her mother and father, who kissed and hugged her as if they would never stop.

The very next day the wedding feast was held. In the great hall of the palace all the lords of the land were assembled. It was a magnificent spectacle. Soon a minstrel, fair as a god, plucked at the strings of his lyre and started to sing. The celebrations had begun. Suddenly, however, the singer broke off in mid-verse and the whole company froze in silent astonishment. For the great doors had burst wide open with a crash and in stalked Phineus, the king's brother, with a troop of soldiers at his heels.

"What is this?" Phineus cried. "You gave your word that she would be my wife. How dare you give her to a stranger!"

"You call me stranger when I saved Andromeda from certain death?" was Perseus' retort. "Besides, her parents gave their oath she would be mine!"

"What?" roared Phineus, "You went back on your sacred word?"

Cepheus and Cassiopeia stood there as if struck dumb.

"Listen to me, all of you," a wise old nobleman declared. "If Andromeda is still alive, it is only because Perseus risked his life to save her. And now Phineus comes to claim his rights. What rights, Phineus? Where were you when Andromeda was chained upon the rock? Why did you not go to kill the monster, but took yourself off without even going to comfort her in her distress? Who broke off the engagement, then, Andromeda's parents or you, by your own cowardice? With what right do you come here now to take her – and by force, as well? Andromeda belongs to Perseus. But should any of you disagree, there's a very simple solution: let's ask the girl herself."

"Yes, ask!" shouted Perseus.

"Ask!" her parents echoed.

"Father," Andromeda said, "my life belongs to the man who saved me. He is the one I shall take as my husband."

"Never!" screamed Phineus. And as the word left his mouth, he flung his spear at Perseus.

The hero had been expecting this. He sprang to one side and was saved. But the shaft lodged in the singer's breast, and as he fell it struck the strings of his lyre which gave out a last melancholy chord and died along with the young man.

Perseus drew his sword to defend himself, while from among the ranks of the guests many brave young men sprang to his side. Battle was joined at once. One after another, Phineus' warriors fell dead upon the ground; but he had a whole army with him, and the struggle soon became unequal as Perseus' supporters were struck down in their turn. Athena herself was alarmed by her hero's plight and came to his assistance, protecting his body with her shield. But the spears and arrows continued to fall like rain around him, and soon not one of Perseus' men was left alive. The brave son of Zeus fought on alone. With his back against a column he carried on a battle with no hope of victory, unless...

Then all at once he shouted:

"Those of you who are my friends, turn your eyes aside!"

And with these words he tore the Medusa's head from its magic wallet and held it up before his enemies. In an instant the warriors of Phineus were transformed into statues, some with their lances poised to throw and others as they charged with sword in hand.

Only Phineus was left. Seeing the fate which had befallen his comrades, he sank in terror at Perseus' feet and begged for mercy. But the hero instantly thrust out the Gorgon's head and turned him, too, to stone. And so Phineus was frozen forever in the most degrading posture a warrior could be caught in – grovelling on his knees and pleading for his life.

Perseus took Andromeda to be his wife. He could not stay long in the palace of Cepheus, however, for it was time for his return to Greece. With tears in her eyes, Andromeda bade farewell to her parents and followed her husband.

When they reached Seriphos, Perseus stopped first at the humble dwelling of Dictys in search of his mother. He opened the door and went in.

"I can't believe it!" cried Dictys when he set eyes on him; and going down on his knees he kissed the hero's hands.

"And you'll believe it even less when you hear I have the Medusa's head," Perseus replied. "But tell me, quickly, how is my mother?"

"The prisoner of Polydectes!" came the answer.

Perseus waited to hear no more, but rushed off in search of the evil king. He found him on a terrace beside the palace, noisily eating and drinking with a group of friends. As soon as Perseus appeared they all rose from their seats in astonishment. Not one of them had ever expected to see his face again, least of all Polydectes.

"How dare you come back here!" he cried, "I sent you to bring the head of the Medusa."

"And I have brought it!"

Polydectes greeted this answer with a mocking laugh. His friends hastened to follow suit, and they all cast scorn on the great hero.

"Listen to that, eh?" they scoffed. "So he's brought the Gorgon's head, has he?" And holding their sides with mirth, they pointed jeering fingers at him.

Then Perseus put his hand into the wallet and pulled out the vile head.

"Here it is," he cried, "since you don't believe me!"

In a flash they were all turned to stone, the mockery stamped forever on their faces. And so, here too, the land was filled with frozen images. If Seriphos is a rocky island today, people say it is because of these stone figures, long since shattered by time and the elements.

As for Phineus and his warriors, there is an even more impressive legend. It is said that in the city of Joppa, in Palestine, men used to point out a spot with a host of tall, upright stones, which the local people claimed were all that was left of Phineus and his troops. A Roman emperor, Marcus Aurelius, took some of those which most resembled men and had them set up in Rome as a reminder to his countrymen of the heroic deeds of Perseus.

But let us get back to our story.

Once Perseus had freed his mother, he made Dictys king of Seriphos and returned to Argos with Danae and Andromeda. As soon as he arrived he gave thanks to Athena for her aid, and presented her with the Gorgon's head, which she placed upon her shield-boss. Then he set off in search of the Stygian nymphs again, to give back the winged sandals, the helmet of Hades and the magic wallet.

By the time he returned to Argos, his grandfather Acrisiüs was nowhere to be found. Fearing that the words of the oracle would at last prove true, he had given up his throne and fled to Larissa, in Thessaly. With his departure, Perseus became king of Argos.

The prophecy comes true

Some time later, a great athletic contest was held in Larissa which attracted contestants from all over Greece. Perseus, too, went to take part in these games, and competed in the discus event. But the hero's throw was so powerful that the discus flew right out of the stadium, struck a passer-by on the head and killed him. That passer-by was none other than Acrisius. And so the words of the oracle were fulfilled: that Acrisius would be killed by his own grandson.

Perseus returned to Argos grieved and ashamed. After what had happened he no longer wished to keep his grandfather's throne, accidental though the killing had been. Luckily, in neighbouring Tiryns, Proetus had been succeeded by his son Megapenthes, and the enmity which had existed between Acrisius and Proetus was only matched by the warmth their successors now showed each other. It was soon agreed that Megapenthes should take the throne of Argos, while Perseus would henceforth rule in Tiryns.

Perseus is also known, however, as the founder and first

ruler of Mycenae, the richest, most glorious and mightiest of all the cities of mythical times. Seeing a good site, not far from Tiryns, the hero decided to fortify the position and transfer his capital there. In the building of Mycenae, Perseus was given great help by the Cyclopes. It is said that only these one-eyed giants could have lifted the great stone blocks that form the fortress walls of Mycenae, and they are known as Cyclopean walls to this very day.

Perseus and Andromeda lived for many years and had seven children. Their eldest child, Perses, became the first king of the Persians, and the founder of that great race. Their second son, Electryon, later became king of Mycenae and it was his daughter, Alcmene, who gave birth to Heracles, the greatest hero in Greek mythology.

As we have seen, all these kings and heroes and founders of dynasties sprang from the line of the river-god Inachus, founder and first king of Argos.

And if we wish to place this great line in order, its members are as follows: first Inachus and next Io, and then Epaphus, followed by Libya, Belus, Danaus, Hypermnestra, Abas, Acrisius and Danae, until we reach the hero Perseus. After him come Electryon and Alcmene and last of all Heracles, the mighty son of Zeus. All in all, there are fourteen generations.

Perseus and Andromeda ruled peacefully over Mycenae, and when they died they did not go to the dark caverns of Hades but were raised into the heavens, for such was the will of great Zeus, Perseus' father. And on a clear night, with the help of a star chart, one can easily find the constellation of Perseus. At its side is Andromeda, and a little further away lie Cepheus and Cassiopeia; for Andromeda died heavy with regret at never having seen her parents again after her marriage, and Zeus, great ruler of the earth and sky, took the couple and placed them in the heavens at their daughter's side.

BELLEROPHON

Sisyphus, Bellerophon's grandfather

Bellerophon was Corinth's greatest hero. His story has thrilled countless generations with its deeds of valour performed as he sailed across the sky upon his great winged horse. Yet it would be a pity to tell his tale without first recounting the myth of his grandfather Sisyphus whose name has also stuck in men's memories, but for the very different reason that he was the most cunning man on earth.

Sisyphus, son of Aeolus, was the founder and first king of Corinth. Though crafty beyond belief, he was not a bad man at heart, yet after his death he was punished harshly, for by his wily tricks he deceived the gods themselves.

When Sisyphus decided to build Corinth, he was attracted to the site near the Isthmus because the new city would thus have two harbours – one on the Gulf of Corinth itself and the other on the Saronic Gulf, with access to the whole Aegean Sea. There was also a tall hill nearby on which he could build an impregnable fortress to shelter the inhabitants of the city in time of war. The site had no water, however, and so Sisyphus begged the river-god Asopus to give him a spring.

"And what will you give me in return?" Asopus asked.

"I have nothing to give you," Sisyphus replied. "But who knows? Perhaps one day you will need me, and then I shall prove a friend."

Satisfied with Sisyphus' answer, Asopus struck the rock with his staff and an abundant stream of clear water gushed out at the foot of the hill before the king's astonished eyes. So Corinth was built, and above it, on the hill, Acrocorinth, the city's fortress.

Some time later, Zeus happened to pass that way, holding by the hand Aegina, the daughter of Asopus. The ruler of gods and men had stolen the girl from her father only a few hours before. Eager to win favour, Sisyphus gave them a warm welcome and the couple spent the night in his palace. But next morning, as soon as they had gone, Asopus arrived, anxiously searching for his daughter and, of course, he asked if Sisyphus had seen her or knew who had taken her away.

Now this put the king of Corinth in a very difficult position. On the one hand he was very much in Asopus' debt, for it was his gift of the spring which had made the founding of Corinth possible – but on the other hand how could he risk anything which might thwart the plans of almighty Zeus? That was the problem! Sisyphus looked at it from every angle, until at last his sense of obligation to Asopus won the day and he told the river-god who had run off with his daughter.

"And do you not now fear the wrath of Zeus?" asked Asopus in admiring wonder.

"Don't worry, I'll find a way out", was Sisyphus' confident reply.

Naturally, when Zeus learned how Asopus had obtained his information he was beside himself with rage.

"The traitor," he roared, "now he will see!" And immediately he ordered Charon to carry off the king's soul to the dark depths of Hades.

However, cunning Sisyphus had already guessed what his fate would be and had set a trap for Charon, whom he awaited with a rope behind his back.

It was not long before the fearsome god of death appeared, but Sisyphus was not dismayed. He threw himself upon him, and before the unsuspecting Charon had any time to react, he found himself bound hand and foot.

Time went by, and while Zeus imagined that Sisyphus had long since received his punishment, Pluto, king of Hades, came unexpectedly to Olympus.

"What are you going to do about Sisyphus?" he enquired, looking very worried.

"My business is with the living, not the dead," said Zeus.

"Exactly," Pluto retorted. "Sisyphus is alive and well – and is making a laughing-stock of us all!"

"What did you say?" growled Zeus.

"Ah, if only that were all," replied Pluto, "But he is

holding Charon prisoner too, and not a soul on earth has perished since. Nobody comes to my kingdom any more!"

Zeus flashed and thundered in his rage and immediately called for Ares, god of war.

"Go to the palace of Sisyphus," he ordered. "Go now, right now. There you will find Charon, bound in chains. Release him, then help him carry off Sisyphus to the kingdom of the dead!"

"Release Charon, yes, that I can understand," was Ares' answer. "But help him in his task? Why, that's unheard of! When did Charon ever need assistance?"

"Well," snapped Zeus, "this time he does. So go and do as I tell you."

Thus poor Sisyphus, who was no match for Charon and Ares combined, soon found himself in the dark halls of Hades.

But since he had been expecting this outcome, too, he had instructed his wife not to make any funeral sacrifices to Pluto on his death. The ruler of the underworld waited in vain for these customary tributes to be paid in his honour, till finally Sisyphus himself appeared before him and said:

"Great lord of Hades, I am deeply grieved that my wife has failed to show you due respect. Let me go up again to earth to punish her and make her pay your sacrifice, as is her duty. As soon as I have done so, I will return to your kingdom."

Pluto was deceived by these persuasive words and allowed Sisyphus to return to the world above, where, of course, instead of punishing his wife as promised, he fell into her arms and lived happily with her to a ripe old age.

But all men must die at last, and when Sisyphus' turn came, the gods took their revenge.

"Now he will see what it costs to make fools of the gods!" Pluto told Zeus. And down in the underworld he set the crafty fellow to work pushing a boulder bigger than himself to the very top of a mountain. Sisyphus strains and sweats to heave that crushing weight up the steep slope, but just before he reaches the summit it always slips from his grasp and rolls down to the valley below. Then he runs panting after it and begins the weary task once more, pushing desperately with hands, shoulders and knees to edge the great rock up the slope. Poor Sisyphus! How he struggles to get that huge stone to the mountain-top and put an

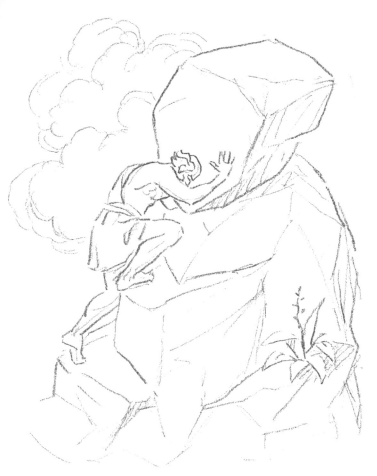

*...but just before he reaches the summit it always slips
from his grasp and rolls down to the valley below...*

end to all his sufferings; but at the last moment it always escapes his grasp and tumbles down the hill once more. His punishment has gone on since the day he died, and it will never cease. Such is the harsh justice meted out to the son of Aeolus, not because he harmed his fellow men, but because he tricked the gods.

Bellerophon and the fatal letter

When Sisyphus died, his son Glaucus became king of Corinth, and Glaucus' son was the hero Bellerophon.

This much-beloved hero was born Hipponous, but the name was soon forgotten when, still a youth, he killed a savage bandit named Bellerus who had become the terror of all Corinth. After this astonishing feat, everyone called him Bellerophon, which means "the slayer of Bellerus."

Now although the people of the city greeted the news of the young hero's feat with relief, the god of war was furious with him and demanded that he be punished. So Bellerophon left Corinth and took himself off to nearby Tiryns, which was then ruled over by Proetus, son of Abas. Proetus welcomed the unlucky youth with warmth, and not only gave him hospitality, but absolved him of all guilt in the killing.

Bellerophon entered the service of the king and carried out the most demanding tasks with such enthusiasm and selflessness that Proetus was amazed.

Unfortunately, the young man's looks – for he was as handsome as a god – attracted the attention of the queen, Stheneboea. Mere admiration soon swelled to uncontrollable desire; and one day, when Proetus was away, she boldly revealed her feelings for the fair young man. Bellerophon resisted her advances, for how could he betray the king who had sheltered him so willingly? It was not in his noble heart to do such a vile thing. The queen's humiliation and resentment were bitter. In an instant her love turned to deadly hatred. Now there was no room in her mind for any thought but how she might contrive his downfall. And in the end she found the way. She approached Proetus and said quite shamelessly:

"Listen, husband, and hear what sort of man you took into your house. Bellerophon has attempted to assault me!"

Proetus was aghast at the news – for however much he respected his young guest it never entered his mind that his wife might be lying.

"Such ingratitude!" he cried.

"Not mere ingratitude, but a mortal insult to us both," his wife continued. "I suppose you realize there is only one way open to you now: kill him or be killed."

These last words of the queen's put Proetus in a sorry dilemma, for the sacred rules of hospitality forbade such punishment for a guest. It was not long, however, before he found a way of fulfilling his wife's wish. Instead of killing the offender with his own hands, he could have it done by Stheneboea's father, king Iobates of Lycia.

And so he sat down and wrote to him as follows:

"The bearer of this letter attempted to dishonour your daughter. See to it that he dies."

Then he sealed the message carefully, handed it to Bellerophon and instructed him to deliver it to Iobates.

The young man innocently took the letter and set off for Lycia.

Presenting himself to the king on his arrival, he handed over Proetus' message. As soon as Iobates learned that Bellerophon had been sent by his son-in-law, he put the letter on one side and received him with feasting and merrymaking which lasted for nine whole days.

Bellerophon tames Pegasus and slays the Chimaera

On the tenth day, Iobates finally remembered to read what Proetus had to say – and as he did so, the smile fled from his lips. The words before him were incredible. This youngster to whom he had just been playing the kind host had shamelessly insulted his daughter!

But although Iobates' instructions were to kill Bellerophon, he had no wish to do so for the same reason which had made Proetus stay his hand. Instead, he thought of a stratagem, and said to the young man:

"Here in our country, a fearsome monster has been wreaking havoc. Its name is the Chimaera, and no man dares to go and hunt it down. If I were your age I would go myself, but I am no longer my old self, and so I thought of you. For I believe you strong and bold enough to do that which I ask of you."

Bellerophon accepted willingly, and Iobates was satisfied that he had found a way of carrying out his son-in-law's instructions – for where he was being sent, the young man would most certainly meet his end.

The Chimaera was a hideous and invincible monster. It had three different heads, being a lion in the front, a dragon at the rear and a goat in the middle. And it was this head which was the most dangerous of all, for it could shoot flames out of its mouth. The Chimaera had spread destruction and death in all the surrounding countryside, not only tearing men and beasts to pieces but scorching planted fields and shady forests too with the fire that spewed forth from its goat-like mouth.

How could such a monster be defeated by strength and determination alone? Realising that these were not enough, Bellerophon went and sought the advice of the wise soothsayer Polyeides.

"The Chimaera," he was told, "can only be defeated by the man who can subdue Pegasus, son of Poseidon – but do not prepare yourself to fight a human opponent, for Pegasus is the winged and immortal horse which sprang from the severed head of the gorgon Medusa when she was slain by Perseus."

"And where can I find Pegasus?" asked Bellerophon.

"All I know is that he roams the mountains and the skies

of Greece," was the reply. "He shuns the company of man, so who can say where he may be found?"

In spite of these faint words of hope, the young man was not discouraged but set off straight away for Greece. On his arrival, he began asking everywhere where Pegasus might be. But all he got for his pains was strange looks.

"We've all heard of this flying horse, but none of us has seen him," said an old man.

"He may just be a fairy tale," replied another.

This set Bellerophon thinking. "If men do not know," he told himself, "perhaps the Nymphs, the Nereids and the Muses may have some idea."

And with this in mind he went to Helicon, the mountain of abundant springs, whose thickly forested slopes were said to conceal a number of these deities. The hero made his way up its wooded flanks, walked through shady valleys, and eventually reached a spring. Ancient plane trees hid the sky and steep rocky cliffs closed in on this enchanted spot, which looked as if it had never felt the touch of feet. But then, above the chuckling of the water and the chirping of the birds, he suddenly heard happy voices and snatches of girlish song. His thoughts flew at once to the

Muses of Helicon; and indeed, in a few moments three lovely maidens as fair as goddesses appeared before him.

"Your face and eyes show us that you have not come to this place with evil intent," they said, "so tell us what you want and perhaps we may help you. For we are the Muses, the daughters of Zeus."

"It is Pegasus I seek," replied Bellerophon boldly.

The Muses looked at him in surprise. "What you ask for is by no means easy, and luck is not with you, either. Had you but come a little sooner, you would have found him here. This spring you see was made by Pegasus, and that is why they call it the Horse spring. He struck his hoof upon the rock and water gushed out at the very spot. But now Pegasus is at Acrocorinth, where there is another fountain he made in the same way. That one is called the Peirene spring. Go there, and you may find him. But keep your distance, for Pegasus does not let any man approach. Yet even should you manage to get near, do not attempt to mount him if you value your life."

The Muses' words were not encouraging, but Bellerophon was undismayed. Satisfied with what little he had learned, he bade farewell to the three maidens and set off for Acrocorinth. The idea of ridding Iobates' kingdom of the dreaded Chimaera filled him with enthusiasm, and the thought of riding Pegasus delighted him so much that it never crossed his mind to count the risks involved.

As Bellerophon was walking towards Acrocorinth, he came upon a temple. It was dedicated to Athena. Going in, he stood before the statue of the goddess, then knelt at its feet and begged for help in finding Pegasus and taming him. Afterwards, since it was late and the sun had already set, he lay down in a sheltered spot outside the temple and quickly fell into a tired sleep. And as he slept he dreamed he saw the goddess Athena herself. In her hands she held a golden bridle.

"Bellerophon, son of Poseidon," the goddess called out to him.

"I am not Poseidon's son," the hero answered in confusion.

"Bellerophon, son of Poseidon," the goddess repeated, "know that Pegasus is your brother, since he, too, has Poseidon for a father. But brother though he may be, he will not let you mount him. Take this bridle, therefore, which has magic powers. Slip it over his head and he will become as docile as a children's pony."

At that very moment Pegasus appeared and came up to Bellerophon, just as if he knew him.

"Be careful not to frighten him," Athena warned. "Put the bridle on him quickly. Splendid. Now stroke his neck and get up on his back. Bravo! You have done it. Pegasus is yours. Farewell – and happy journey!"

It was unbelievable. Bellerophon was soaring through the air on Pegasus' back. It was enchanting! – but an enchantment that was neither real nor long-lasting, for soon the hero woke up to find himself still lying on the ground.

Disappointed that it had only been a dream, he got to his feet, but as he did so he saw a bridle by his side. It was the very same golden bridle the goddess had given him as he slept. He took the precious object in his hands. This time his eyes were not deceiving him. It was no dream. He really was holding the bridle with which he could tame Pegasus.

Bellerophon immediately set off again for Acrocorinth. He soon found the spring named Peirene, where he hid behind a bush and waited. With every rustling of the leaves his head jerked round in the hope that he would see the

..."Be careful not to frighten him," Athena warned...

horse he had come so far to find. Then suddenly a strange beating sound made him look up in the sky – and there was Pegasus. He was a splendid snow-white beast with broad wings which carried him through the air with all the grace of a swan. Bellerophon gazed at him in awe. But he soon realized that he would have to hide himself more securely, and crouched deeper under the bush. In a few moments Pegasus came to earth, right in front of the concealed hero.

The horse could not see Bellerophon, but he sensed at once that someone was nearby and glared around him, neighing fiercely and raising his wings in a threatening way. Bellerophon was not alarmed by this, but waited quietly for the right moment. Pegasus, however, showed no sign of calming down, so Bellerophon picked up a stone and threw it over the horse's back into a bush. Hearing the noise, Pegasus swung his head round and with ears pricked taut, tried to make out where the sound had come from. For an instant he was standing completely motionless. Quick as lightning, Bellerophon sprang from his hiding place and before Pegasus had time to move a muscle he had slipped the bridle over his nose. The startled horse turned to see the young man gently stroking his neck, but holding the bridle fast. Then, realizing what had happened, he made no attempt to pull free, but gave a friendly and submissive neigh. The proud wild creature had been broken in.

Bellerophon led the now docile Pegasus to the spring and when they had both drunk he mounted on its back. Responding to his gentle tug at the bit, the horse unfolded his great white wings and bore Bellerophon high into the heavens. The dream had come true!

Pulling on the reins as he guided Pegasus across the sky, the young man wished this marvellous flight might never end. His lungs were filled with bracing air and his eyes drank in the magnificent spectacle which revealed itself as the earth unfolded beneath him, with its pattern of tree-clad mountains, rivers glinting in the sun and island-studded seas. Winging through the air like a god, with the clouds for his companions, the hero felt a swelling strength within him.

It did not take them long to reach Lycia. Bellerophon's keen eyes searched all around for some sign which would tell him where the Chimaera had its dwelling. Soon they saw below a barren stretch of land without a single tree, and the hero brought Pegasus down lower to get a better view. There was not a blade of grass in sight, only charred trunks which stood up here and there; and among them lay the bones of animals, and sometimes even of men. It was clear that the monster's home must lie nearby. And at that very moment, sensing an intruder, the Chimaera came out of its lair. Pegasus and his rider spotted the hideous monster at once, for they were flying at no great height. Bellerophon was not afraid, but Pegasus soared skyward – and luckily he did so, for the Chimaera immediately began to belch flames from its goat-like mouth, and had these touched the horse and rider, both would have been lost. Seeing they had escaped, the monster grew more vicious still and let out a series of terrifying roars and hisses, while its flames shot out to their fullest extent, lighting up the cloudy skies like thunderbolts, as if some savage storm had broken.

Not even this struck fear into Bellerophon's heart. Pulling on Pegasus' reins he soared higher than the flames could reach. Now his moment had come. With calm and steady movements he unslung the bow from his shoulder, drew

...Bellerophon took careful aim and shot...

an arrow from its sheath, bent back the bow with all his force, took careful aim and shot. A sharp whistle cleaved the air, immediately followed by a hideous scream which showed the arrow had not gone astray. Quickly, Bellerophon pulled out another shaft and shot again. Then another, and another, and each was followed by a howl of agony from the Chimaera as proof that every bolt was striking home. Unable to retaliate, the monster was a target for so many arrows that it gave one final spasm, then sank down dead upon the ground. The invincible Chimaera had been defeated.

Bellerophon's other feats

When Iobates saw Bellerophon alive and well and heard his news, he was both angry and frustrated. But instead of letting these feelings show, he said:

"Well done, my lad! You are a hero now." And then, after a moment's thought, he added:

"If you serve me faithfully and do mighty deeds, you will win great glory – and I shall honour and reward you as you deserve. Go now, therefore, and sweep Mount

Tmolos clean of the bandits which infest it."

"I shall go," replied the hero; and Iobates rejoiced, for he was sure that this time Bellerophon would not escape his fate.

The hero mounted upon Pegasus and set off. However, instead of the few bandits he had imagined, he found a whole tribe of bloodthirsty warriors. All the soldiers in Lycia could not have put them down. But Bellerophon defeated the ruffians by swooping low over their heads on Pegasus, killing the most fearsome of them and scattering the rest. And they never troubled the region again.

When the hero returned, Iobates was angrier than ever. Yet he was still determined to destroy him, and this time he decided to send Bellerophon to do battle with the Amazons, sure that anyone who tried his strength against these formidable women warriors would never come back alive. Yet to Iobates' utter amazement, Bellerophon returned victorious once more.

The king had only one card left to play. He ordered the roughest bunch of fighters in Lycia, the much-feared Xanthian warriors, to lay an ambush for the hero and cut him down.

Bellerophon was on foot, taking a walk on the banks of the river Xanthus, when the warriors sent by Iobates sprang out upon him. Never in his life had the hero been in such mortal danger as that which faced him now. It was clear that he could never hold his own against so many – but in that instant he remembered that Athena had addressed him as 'son of Poseidon', and he called on that mighty god of the sea to bring him aid. The moment he did so, a strange thing happened: the waters of the river Xanthus rose from their bed and came surging up behind Bellerophon. As he advanced, so did the waters, and whenever he stopped, so did they. Seeing this miracle, Iobates' warriors were seized with fear and began to draw back, but Bellerophon moved on against them with ever-quickening pace. The waters rolled forward at his heels – and the Xanthian warriors fled in terror. But the hero was in close pursuit, and behind him came the foaming waves of the angry river. Now he was nearing the city. Iobates saw all this and could not believe his eyes. If the city and the plain were flooded, it would be a disaster beyond description. Already an anxious crowd had gathered. Iobates, most anxious of them all, called out to the warriors:

"Cowards! Stop him! We shall all be drowned!" But such was the panic that had seized them that they scattered in all directions and were soon lost to sight.

The truth revealed

Now if the men were not ashamed to take to their heels, their wives and daughters certainly were, and one of them shouted:

"Advance with me, women of Xanthus; let us wipe out this stain our brave menfolk have left upon our honour!"

And immediately they sprang forward to face the hero. Now Bellerophon had no wish to harm these women or their city, and he was ready to retreat. But Athena urged him on. She had her plan, and so he continued his advance.

When only a short distance now separated them, the women stopped and one of them cried out:

"Choose whichever of us you desire, and take her for your wife – or kill her if you will – but do not flood our land!"

Bellerophon did not reply. He walked steadily on towards them, and the foaming waters followed in his wake.

Now he was very close, but the Xanthian women did not retreat an inch. On came the hero, and with him came the waters; and the women, not knowing what else to do, lifted high their skirts – as if the only thing that concerned them was keeping their clothes dry, and as if lifted skirts would save them from the roaring waves of a whole mighty river.

And yet they did save them, and all the city, too. For believe it or not, as soon as Bellerophon caught sight of the women's thighs he blushed to the very roots of his hair and turned back in confusion. At the same instant the waters rolled back, too, and returned to the bed of the river Xanthus.

Iobates, who had witnessed everything, was astonished beyond words. A sudden doubt was planted in his mind, and grew there till all at once he asked himself:

"But how could the man who assaulted my own daughter without shame have blushed at the mere sight of a woman's thighs?"

Then at last the truth dawned on him.

"It was all a lie," he shouted. "Bellerophon is innocent!"

And he immediately ran to find the hero, clutching Proetus' letter in his hand.

"Read it!" he commanded.

When Bellerophon saw its contents he was speechless.

"This is why I sent you to carry out such dangerous tasks," Iobates explained. "I believed a lie. But why did Proetus write this, I would like to know?"

"What purpose will it serve to learn the reason why?" Bellerophon replied. "In any case, Proetus is not to blame – and nor is anybody, for that matter. It is the gods who guide the hands of mortals."

After that, Iobates asked no more questions. Perhaps he had already guessed the truth, for now he respected the hero even more; so much so, indeed, that he gave Bellerophon his youngest daughter, Philonoë, in marriage and made him his heir.

Nor did Iobates forget the great service the Xanthian women had rendered to his city – or the cowardice of his 'bold' warriors. In remembrance, he decided to bring back an ancient custom. He decreed that the inhabitants of the regions neighbouring on the river Xanthus should cease naming their children after their fathers, but should call them by their mothers' names instead. And so, in those parts, a boy was not called, say, 'Alcaeus, son of Jason', but 'Alcaeus, son of Daphne', which in those days was considered a great honour for the women and an equally great humiliation for their menfolk.

On the death of Iobates, Bellerophon became king of Lycia. His wife bore him two sons and a daughter, Laodameia, whose beauty was such that Zeus himself loved her, and by him she had Sarpedon, a great hero who met a glorious death in the Trojan war.

Bellerophon lived happily for many years, and with the help of Pegasus performed other wonderful exploits which spread his fame as king and hero even further.

The sad fall of Bellerophon

But however good and brave a man may be, he often falls from grace before the end; for power and glory breed a pride that can make a man lose all sense of his proper place.

Bellerophon was flattered by the love and admiration which his people showered on him; and whenever he mounted on Pegasus and soared over the towns and cities of his land, he would feel a glow of satisfaction to think that here he was, doing a thing no other man could even dream of. As he sailed through the heavens, his mind would dwell on what Athena had told him in his sleep: that he was the son of Poseidon; till in the end he came to think himself the equal of the gods, and that his rightful place was not on earth but Olympus. And so, one day, he leapt on Pegasus and set course for the dwelling of the gods. In the blindness of his pride, he imagined that his father would be waiting for him at the gates and would seat him at his side before the table of the gods. He even pictured Hebe coming to fill his cup with the nectar that would make him an immortal.

Filled with these vain and foolish ideas, Bellerophon flew higher still and higher, up above the clouds, until at last he saw before him, jutting from that fleecy sea, the towering mass of Mount Olympus, and on its peak the imposing palaces of the gods, gleaming in the sun.

But even as Bellerophon's vain spirit swelled with self-importance, he was spotted from on high by mighty Zeus himself.

"What insolence is this?" cried the lord of gods and men. "A mortal approaches Olympus, and uninvited, too!"

And with these words he launched a giant horsefly against Pegasus. One bite from the venomous insect was enough. Pegasus let out a loud neigh of agony and went wild. Beating his great wings madly in his desperate pain, he bucked and reared so violently that in the end he threw Bellerophon from his back.

From his high seat in the heavens, the hero plummeted earthwards. Athena saw his fall and hastened to his aid in anxious pity; but though she saved Bellerophon from death, his mind was turned forever.

"Alas!" the goddess mourned. "Why does glory go straight to men's heads? What could be nobler than earthly power wielded in a humble spirit? If only all men could understand this! What a fair and worthy man Bellerophon once was – and look at him now, wandering the earth without a place to go to or even knowing what he's doing. And I am powerless to help. Alas, alas!"

And so Bellerophon stumbled on aimlessly wherever his footsteps took him, forgotten by his fellow men and abandoned by the gods, until at last death crossed his path.

The hero's body was found by the Muses, those divine maidens who had long ago helped him to find Pegasus.

They gently lifted up the lifeless form, washed it, dressed it in funeral clothes and buried it on a quiet slope of Olympus, weeping bitter tears.

Time went by, but the Muses did not forget Bellerophon, and nor did they allow the memory of his deeds to be lost to men for ever. By inspiring poets and singers, they soon restored the fame of his great feats and filled men's hearts with an even greater love for the hero who tamed Pegasus and slew the fearsome Chimaera.

Melampus

But now that the tale of Bellerophon is ended, let us go back in time and space to Tiryns, to the palace of king Proetus. Stheneboea was fated to pay dearly for the wicked lie she had told about the hero. A kinsman of Iobates arrived from Lycia and told the whole story to her furious husband.

"Woman!" spat Proetus. "You're rotten to the core! Get out of here – and let me never set eyes on you again!"

Thus, in an instant, Stheneboea's world collapsed in ruins. Where was now her life of grandeur and high rank?

In her despair, she found no place to turn. To go back to her father was impossible; to become a beggar when she had known the honours paid to queens was more than she could bear. And so she left, not knowing where to hide her face. It was a length of rope lying in her path which offered the way out, and she clutched it to her bosom like a precious thing. A little further on there stood a tree. Her end was swift and nasty, fitting payment for her vile falsehood.

But for Proetus, too, who had hounded Bellerophon unjustly, without ever questioning his guilt, there were hard days to come. His two daughters, Lysippe and Iphianassa, went mad. After both father and daughters had gone through untold sufferings, they were finally made well again by a wise seer and healer named Melampus, a man who had acquired almost magical powers, and in the strangest way.

One day, Melampus saw an eagle swoop down on a serpents' nest. The parents were putting up a desperate struggle in defence of their young, and out of the kindness of his heart, Melampus ran to chase the bird of prey away. But he was too late to save the grown snakes from the eagle's cruel beak, and so he sadly buried them nearby and

...Melampus ran to chase the bird of prey away...

then lay down to sleep. While he slept, the young snakes came, and out of gratitude they licked his ears clean with their tongues. From that moment, Melampus was able to understand the speech of wild creatures and it was this power that enabled him to become a seer and great healer.

Now Melampus had a brother, Bias, to whom he was deeply attached. When Bias fell in love with Pero, daughter of king Neleus of Pylos, the seer was eager to help him win her for his wife. Neleus, however, would only give his daughter to the man who brought him the splendid cattle of Phylacus, whose strength and beauty made him long to be their owner. But nobody could lay their hands on the animals, for Phylacus kept them safely shut up in a strong-walled pen at Phylace, where they were guarded night and day by dogs and men. Thanks to his special powers, Melampus knew that he could obtain the beasts – if he was ready to spend a year in jail as the price for them. Much as he loved his brother and had helped him in the past, this was too high a price to pay, and so he gently advised Bias to give up all thought of marrying Pero.

From the day he heard these words, Bias fell into a deep melancholy. He lost his appetite, could not sleep a wink and thought only of the lovely daughter of Neleus who would never be his wife.

When Melampus saw his brother in this hopeless state he realized that he would have to play the cattle thief after all. But, as he had foreseen, he had scarcely jumped over the wall of their enclosure when he was seized by Phylacus himself.

"Two things I value in this world," growled Phylacus, "first my son Iphiclus, and next to him my cattle. And so it's jail for you – and don't expect me to set you free again."

Almost a year had passed when Melampus heard two woodworms talking as they gnawed away at the great beam which held up the roof of his cell.

"How much work is left to do, brother?" asked one of them.

"If we don't waste our time in idle conversation, the beam will fall tomorrow morning," replied the other, his mouth full of wood dust.

As soon as he heard this, Melampus began demanding in alarm to be transferred to another cell; and Phylacus, who did not sleep a wink that night for his prisoner's shout-ing, was obliged to give in to Melampus' demands next morning.

To his utter astonishment, the seer was hardly through the door when the roof collapsed behind him.

"I had heard you were a mighty seer and healer," said Phylacus, "but I never believed it – till now, that is. Consider yourself a free man, and take the cattle, too; only cure my unhappy son Iphiclus and make him able to give his wife a child."

The next day Melampus sacrificed to Apollo and sought his aid in restoring Iphiclus' manhood.

Help came immediately. Two vultures wheeled down from the sky and settled on a nearby tree. Presently, Melampus heard one of them remark:

"Do you recall the last time we were here, and saw Phylacus slaughtering rams in sacrifice to Apollo?"

"Of course I do," replied the other, "but that must have been years ago. His son Iphiclus was still a child then, and I remember how terrified he was when he saw his father coming towards him with the bloody knife. It gave the poor boy such a shock it quite unmanned him. Why, even now, he cannot father a child."

"I know," said the first vulture. "But do you remember,

too, that his father stuck the knife into the trunk of a tree when he ran to comfort the boy? Look carefully, and you'll see the knife is still there! You can just make out its handle; over the years the bark has almost covered it."

"Why, so it is – and here's how Iphiclus can be healed. Since it was the knife that harmed him, the knife can make him well again. But someone will have to pull it from the trunk and use the rust from its blade to make the medicine which will give Iphiclus back his manly strength."

"Just as you say," nodded the first vulture, "but who knows the art of healing as well as we; and who understands our words for us to tell him what to do?"

But, of course, Melampus had heard and understood every word they said, and in his gratitude he tossed two scraps of entrails to the vultures, who seized them in their beaks and flapped heavily away, pleased to know that they had not sat waiting in the tree so long to no avail.

As soon as they were gone, Melampus drew the old knife from the tree and with its rust he mixed a medicine that worked wonders. Iphiclus' strength was restored, and his wife bore him a son whom they named Podarces. Delighted with the healer's treatment, Phylacus gave Melampus the cattle just as he had promised. The seer drove the animals off to Bias, who joyfully handed them over to Neleus and received the lovely Pero in exchange.

This cure, and many others, made Melampus famous for his healing far and wide. So when Proetus' daughters lost their wits, the king naturally called on him for help; and he had even decided to pay the healer handsomely, although he was normally the very spirit of stinginess.

Now Melampus knew, and frowned on, the king's lack of generosity, and to provoke him said:

"I will make your daughters well – but only if you give me a third of your kingdom in return."

Proetus almost choked when he heard this outrageous fee – but Melampus had not finished with him yet.

"It's not a lot to ask," he smiled, "especially when you consider I'll be curing you of your meanness, too!"

"Get out of here, you robber!" Proetus screamed. "Doctors like you are two a penny!"

But, of course, he found no one capable of curing his daughters; and what is more, their illness began to spread to the other women of Tiryns. What could the king do but call for Melampus again, only to hear this time:

"I see the number of victims has risen – and so has my fee. I shall now want a third of your kingdom for myself, and another third for my brother, Bias. And if you quibble about the price, you'll soon be left without a sane woman in your kingdom."

Furious with himself for dismissing the healer's original offer, Proetus now saw that he had no choice but to give up another third as well, and grudgingly accepted.

Melampus first asked the king what had brought the sickness on, and what he learned proved as serious as he had feared.

It was Hera who had driven the women of Tiryns mad, because Proetus' daughters had not gone to offer sacrifice to her at the great festival called the Heraion, in the city of Argos. The task that now faced Melampus was to coax the goddess into restoring the unhappy women's sanity. And this was not just a difficult task, but a seemingly impossible one; for when Hera's rage was roused, neither men nor gods could pacify her – except, perhaps, for Artemis. Surely Hera would not refuse the goddess of the hunt, who had done her numerous favours recently. The two of them had been working hand in hand of late, punishing all who did

them harm. Yet how could Artemis be persuaded to inter-
cede on behalf of Proetus' daughters when she, like Hera,
knew only how to take revenge, not seek forgiveness? Here
was another problem, still more difficult than the first, but
once more, Melampus found the answer.

"The sun god, Helios, could ask her," the seer thought.
"He's a kindhearted fellow, and if I offer him a rich enough
sacrifice, he'll take pity on these poor mad women and
beg Artemis to cure them. She may refuse at first, but he'll
know a way of making her relent."

Sure enough, Helios took up the case as eagerly as
Melampus had wished.

"Listen, Artemis," said the sun god, "I want you to ask
Hera to lift this madness from the daughters of Proetus
and the other women of Tiryns. They have been punished
quite enough."

"Ask me to punish," Artemis replied, "and I will do it
gladly – but go and ask for mercy? No, that I will never
do. The human race must learn to fear the gods."

Now Helios had expected the goddess to refuse, and
knew just how to answer. .

"If you deny me this favour," he warned, "then I shall

not reveal to you what I see on my journeys across the heavens; and then you will no longer know who owes you sacrifices still unpaid. And so, little by little, the human race will cease to fear you altogether."

This threat touched Artemis to the quick. What could she do but go and beg to Hera, who had no choice but to grant her wish. Melampus' wisdom had borne fruit yet again: the daughters of Proetus and all the other women of Tiryns were cured of their madness and became their old selves once more.

Melampus and his brother Bias, whose wife had meanwhile died and left him alone in the world again, now went off in search of Proetus' daughters and found them in a cave in Arcadia. When the two girls were strong enough to travel, they took them back to their father, who wept tears of joy at seeing them completely recovered and as lovely as goddesses once more, just as they had been before their illness.

"There is just one other thing, however," Melampus informed Proetus. "I have achieved the impossible, and so I am afraid that my fee will be rather higher than agreed. I shall now want your daughters, as well: Lysippe for myself, and Iphianassa for my brother Bias."

This time, Proetus could not have been happier. He swept the two brothers into his arms and embraced them warmly.

"I shall give you all my kingdom, too," he promised. "I am an old man now, and all I want is a quiet corner where I can fade peacefully away."

"Didn't I tell you I would cure you of your meanness?" Melampus replied. And the others laughed so much he could hardly make himself heard.

The wedding ceremonies took place shortly after. Melampus and Bias took Proetus' lovely daughters for their brides, and the kingdom of Tiryns they shared between them.

THESEUS, THE HERO OF ATHENS

The birth of Theseus

Aegeus, son of Pandion, was a king of Athens who is chiefly remembered because he is said to have been the father of the renowned hero Theseus – though whether

Theseus really was his son is a matter of dispute.

When Aegeus married, his dearest wish was to have a son to succeed him on the throne of Athens. But the years rolled by and still his wife had not borne him a single child. So desperate was he for a son that he remarried, again without result. Finally he decided to go to Delphi to learn at the oracle of Apollo what he must do to gain the son he yearned for.

The answer of Apollo's priestess was mysterious:

"Ruler of men, do not untie your wineskin until you reach the Acropolis of Athens."

Bewildered by this warning, Aegeus left the Delphic oracle even more melancholy than he had come.

"What sort of an answer was that?" he asked himself. "I can't make head or tail of it!" Granted, he did not open the bulging wineskin he was carrying, but how could that help solve his problem? As he made his way home, he puzzled over how to make the oracle's message give up its meaning.

"I shall go by way of Corinth and ask Medea," he decided in the end.

Medea was the most powerful sorceress the world had

ever known. Jason had brought her with him from the distant Caucasus when he went to win the golden fleece, but now, found guilty of a hideous crime, she lived alone in a wretched hut outside the walls of Corinth, shunned by all. Thus it seemed most strange to her to see a man actually crossing her threshold.

Aegeus gave her a friendly greeting, told her he was returning from Delphi and that he had been there to consult the oracle, and finally recounted the priestess's message.

Now Medea was not only a mighty sorceress, but no mean soothsayer either. Even so, the oracle's words were beyond her power to fathom, save for the fact that she knew at once Aegeus would never be able to father a son. Then, after a moment's thought, she said:

"I can give you an heir, though only by means of magic. However, I shall want my reward – and that will be for you to take me for your wife and make me queen of Athens."

Such was Aegeus' longing for a child that in his delight he agreed at once and would have taken Medea with him there and then, had she not said:

"I will not come with you now. First I must work my magic. Go to your palace, prepare the wedding feast, and send for me when all is ready. But return to Athens by way of Troezen."

Aegeus, who could not understand why Medea would not come with him, began to doubt her word.

"Is she playing with me?" he wondered. "Anyway, I'll take the road she said. It will give me an opportunity to visit old Pittheus, the wise king of Troezen. Perhaps he can explain the oracle's words to me."

Pittheus, the son of Pelops and Hippodameia, was the wisest man ever to be born into this world. Some even said that he was wiser than the centaur Cheiron.

Pittheus gave the king of Athens a warm welcome and Aegeus told him of his sorrows and the strange words of the priestess.

For the first time in his life, the old man found himself presented with an oracle he could not explain at once. He gave the problem much deep thought, worked out various conjunctions of symbols, numbers and stars and finally, looking very pleased with himself, announced:

"The meaning of the oracle is that you will be granted

an heir to the throne, that he will become the most renowned of all Athenian heroes, and that his name will be remembered for all eternity."

Seeing Aegeus beside himself with joy, Pittheus thought of his only daughter, Aethra – and what went through his mind put a happy smile on his face.

Years before, when Aethra was still a little girl, he had promised her to Bellerophon as a bride. But Bellerophon had left for Lycia and had not been heard of for a long time now. Once a girl was betrothed, however, that was the end of the matter. According to the custom of those days, she no longer had the right to marry another man.

This state of affairs had given Pittheus much grief; but now, he had found a solution.

"Since my Aethra can never know the happiness of marriage," he told himself, "she might at least experience the joy of motherhood. Let her become the mother of the hero the oracle foretold, and I will take care of them both."

And so, half-joking but half in earnest, he said to Aegeus:

"Do you know why the priestess told you not to open the wineskin you have with you? So we can open mine, which holds the finest vintage in the world."

And he ran to fill a jug and pour it into the cups which stood before them. "Good health to you, friend Aegeus," he said, "and believe me, your wish will be granted."

"I believe it will," replied Aegeus, thirstily drinking the wine down in a single gulp. "I can feel it coming."

"You can indeed," agreed Pittheus, refilling his cup with a crafty smile.

Now this wine was not only delicious but very strong as well; by the end of his second cup, Aegeus no longer knew what he was saying or doing. In that state, half carrying him on his shoulder, Pittheus led him into his daughter's bedchamber.

When Aegeus awoke in the morning and the fumes had cleared from his head, he was surprised to find he had spent the night with Aethra, but not displeased when he realized what had happened.

"Medea has kept her promise!" he exclaimed. "I shall acquire a son by magic means, and he will be the greatest hero of Athens!"

And after a moment's thought he said to Aethra:

"I believe you will bear me a son, and this gives me great joy. But there is something you must do. Come, I will show you."

With these words, he took Aethra by the hand and led her to a great stone. Although he was a man of formidable strength, it took him all his powers to lift it, for it was a huge boulder. Then he placed beneath it a sword and a pair of sandals, saying:

"This sword I lay beneath the rock is a family heirloom. It was the weapon worn by Cecrops, first king of Athens. The sandals are mine. When my son is sixteen years of age, tell him to come and seek me out. But first he must lift this boulder, take the sword and sandals from beneath it and wear them so that I may recognise him. Then I shall be doubly proud, knowing he is my son and has the strength to lift this great rock, too."

But Medea had known what she was saying. Aegeus would never father a child of his own – and yet the heir to the throne of Athens was destined to be born. He would not be Aegeus' son, though, but the offspring of the union of Aethra with Poseidon, the great god of the sea. This, however, the king of Athens would never learn.

Thanks to Medea's magic, the goddess Athena came to Aethra in her sleep and said:

"Rise and go to Sphaeria, the round island off the shore, and offer sacrifice in memory of Myrtilus, the charioteer who made possible the marriage between your forebears Pelops and Hippodameia."

Aethra obeyed, but, at the place the goddess said, she found Poseidon waiting for her. He dragged her into a cave and made her his own. The magic of Medea had done its work. And thus, nine months later, in a little cove near Troezen, Aethra gave birth to the sea god's son – although it was given out that Aegeus was the father. The boy's name was Theseus.

In honour of Athena, Aethra later built a small temple in the place of her union with Poseidon. It was called the temple of Deceiving Athena because of the goddess's part in that night's work; and ever since, the little island has been called the Sacred Isle.

Theseus grew up at Troezen in the care of his mother and watched over by his wise old grandfather. From his earliest youth his intelligence and energy set him apart, and as for his strength and daring, the following tale is told:

One day, Heracles came to visit Pittheus and tossed his

lion's pelt on a couch head upwards, so that from the door it looked as if it were a real live lion. Shortly afterwards, some boys came into the room, and as soon as they saw the lion's head they took to their heels in panic. Among them was Theseus. He had not run away in fear however, but to fetch an axe with which to kill the 'beast'. And at this time he was only seven years old.

Old Pittheus himself saw to the teaching of the lad, and from him Theseus learned literature, sciences and the arts. To exercise his body and make him quick and strong, he called in the most famous gymnasts of the day, and the son of Aethra was soon capable of handling any danger that might arise.

Theseus' feats on the dangerous road to Athens

The years rolled by and Theseus was growing into manhood. Soon he was sixteen and his mother led him to the rock.

"Beneath that rock," she told him, "there lie a sword and a pair of sandals. They were placed here by your father Aegeus, king of Athens. Now you must roll the stone aside, take them, put them on and go to Athens to present yourself before your father. He will know you are his son from the sword and sandals that you wear."

Theseus was now an impressively burly lad; and so he rolled the stone aside with ease, picked up the sandals and laced them to his feet, buckled on the belt, then threw his mother a look of shy pride.

Aethra gazed at her son in admiration, for thus clad he seemed as handsome as a god. Then she kissed him twice, her eyes filling with tears. The hour for them to part was drawing near.

Both his mother and old Pittheus advised the boy to make his way to Athens by sea.

"The land route via the Isthmus is swarming with robbers and bandits," they warned him. "Only the ignorant go that way – and they never survive the journey."

"If that's the case, then it's the land route I must take," replied Theseus decisively. Pittheus and Aethra pleaded with him in vain; and it was on foot that he set out for Athens.

He had not reached neighbouring Epidaurus before he encountered his first bandit, a villain named Periphetes who

...Theseus rolled the stone aside with ease...

held a great bronze cudgel. Since he was in the habit of using this to kill every unfortunate traveller who passed that way, he had earned the nickname "Cudgelman." Theseus saw him planted in the middle of the road, tall and fearsome as a giant, but he seemed quite undismayed and did not even slow his pace. Indeed, when he drew close enough he even had the boldness to cry out:

"Stand aside and let me pass!"

"When I am standing on this road," growled the bandit, "no one goes a step further – or a step back, for that matter; I kill him where he stands. This bronze club which I hold was forged by Hephaestus himself; no one escapes its blow. And now the time has come for you to try it on your head!" So saying, he swung the cudgel in the air with all his awful strength to strike young Theseus down.

Swift as a tiger, the young man leapt upon him, snatched the terrible weapon from his hands and dealt the villain such a blow with his own cudgel that he dropped dead on the spot. "No one escapes its blow," Periphetes had boasted – and neither had he. Pleased with the outcome of his first encounter, the young man shouldered the bronze cudgel and continued on the road to Athens.

Near the Isthmus of Corinth was a stretch where the road wound through a pine forest, and here Theseus met his second bandit, Sinis, or 'pine-bender' as he was known, because of the hideous way he killed unlucky passers-by. With his great muscles he would bend two trees to the ground, then tie one of his victim's legs to the top of each. Having done this, he would release the trees, which sprang upright again, tearing the poor traveller in two.

And this was what Sinis planned to do to Theseus.

"Look how strong I am!" he said, forcing a pine tree to the ground.

"Do you have the strength to hold it down?" – for he saw how muscular the young man was.

"I do," said Theseus, holding on to it.

"Now I shall bend this one," he said, heaving on another tree. Suddenly Theseus realized what his fate would be, although he had not seen the trick at first. Seizing the bandit in his powerful grasp, he snatched the rope which Sinis carried at his waist and in a trice had lashed his two feet to the tree tops. Then he released them skywards, condemning the villain to the same hideous death he had meted out to so many unsuspecting wayfarers.

Further along the road to Athens, Theseus came to a village of onion growers named Crommyum. The people of this place were in despair.

"A terrible wild boar is laying waste our land," they told him. "It has rooted up the whole valley with its snout, and nothing will grow in our fields. We and our families shall starve – for this is no ordinary boar, but a vile monster, the child of Typhoon and Echidna, and all who go to face it meet their death."

"Then I shall kill it," said Theseus. And without another word he strode off across the broad plain in search of the fearsome beast.

None of the villagers believed the brave young man had any chance of killing a wild boar such as this; so when, next day, they saw Theseus coming back across the plain, they could not imagine what it was he was carrying on his shoulders. Their mouths dropped open in astonishment when he arrived and dumped the lifeless carcass of the monster at their feet.

Overcome with gratitude, the villagers surrounded the young hero and tried to thank him. But Theseus was anxious to be on his way, and as soon as they would let him he set off once again for Athens.

A little further on, he reached the famous pass which is today called the Perilous Steps. In those days there was just a narrow pathway cut out of the rock, backed by the towering peaks and falling sheer down to the sea below.

In modern times a road has been carved through and cars go speeding past, but in those distant times the pass was so dangerous that many travellers preferred to climb the mountain and come down the other side rather than risk that perilous way where one false step meant death.

This pass was known to the ancients as Sciron's Rocks – for as if the pathway itself were not dangerous enough, it was also the haunt of an evil-doer named Sciron who killed those bold enough to attempt the crossing in the strangest and most cunning way.

Sciron would force every traveller he met to sit and wash his feet, making him perform this task seated on the edge of the precipice with his back towards the sea. And as soon as the stranger had completed this humiliating labour, instead of thanking him, Sciron would give a mighty kick and send him tumbling to the sea below, where a gigantic turtle was always waiting and devoured him in an instant.

This was the fate that Sciron had in store for Theseus.

"If you wish to pass, you must first wash my feet," he told him roughly.

"All right, I'll wash them," replied Theseus. "But this time it won't turn out as you imagine!"

"We shall see how it turns out in just a moment," growled Sciron and extended his foot to be washed by the stranger, who, being so young, had not impressed him overmuch.

"Yes, we shall see!" said Theseus – and with astonishing strength he seized the foot the bandit offered him and flung him from the rock. Sciron went hurtling to the sea below, where the waiting turtle swallowed him in one gulp. And so the heartless killer paid for his victims' lives in the same coin he had asked of them – death.

Pleased with his feat at Sciron's Rocks, Theseus continued on his way. He had nearly reached Eleusis when he found another mortal danger facing him. This time he had to pit his skills against Cercyon, a formidable wrestler who cornered all who came his way and made them fight him to the death. Not one of those who had fought with him till now had lived to tell the tale. When Cercyon saw Theseus was just a lad, he sneered at him and said:

"Is there no man worthy of the name but me? I'm tired of killing youths and weaklings!"

"And what gives you the idea that you're a worthy man?" Theseus retorted angrily. "Since when have common criminals been worthy?"

"Not only young, but insolent as well," said Cercyon in a provoking tone.

"Call me insolent, if you like. Call me ill-bred, too – if you ever get the chance!"

And with these words he threw himself on the bandit, grasped him by the legs, raised him high into the air, then dashed him to the ground so violently that he was killed outright.

After this trial of strength Theseus crossed Mount Aegaleo and began the downhill stretch which would lead him into Athens. But at Corydallus, yet another villain, Procrustes, was waiting for a victim. As soon as he saw Theseus he stopped him. Nearby, the young hero saw a bloodstained bed.

"Come and lie down," Procrustes offered.

But the young hero knew what his fate would be if he lay down on that bed. For on it Procrustes used to bind his victims and kill them in a hideous way. If anyone was too short for the bed, he would pull him till his body stretched to fit it, heaving with all his terrible strength until his unfortunate victim died in agony. If, on the other hand, the bed was too short for the guest, Procrustes would simply take out a saw and cut him down to size!

"Lie down and have a rest," Procrustes offered once again.

Theseus did not waste time declining, but seized him in a powerful embrace, raised him in the air and flung him on the bed. And since Procrustes was a massive fellow, and far too long for it, Theseus dealt him the same treatment that had been meted out to so many innocent travellers in the past.

This was the last brave deed that Theseus performed on the road to Athens. Already the city was in sight, its acropolis crowned by the temple of Athena.

In Athens

Now Theseus was walking along the Sacred Way. Near the bridge which spanned the Cephissus some small houses stood on the river bank. These were the dwellings of the Phytalids, simple and hardworking people whose forebear, Phytalus, was said to have been the most hospitable man who ever walked the earth. He had even welcomed the goddess Demeter into his home in the course of her anguished wanderings in search of her daughter Persephone.

The warmth of hospitality still ran in his descendants' blood, and the Phytalids would never let a traveller cross the river without inviting him to rest and let them tend to his needs. And thus they welcomed Theseus, too.

When they were seated at table and Theseus had told them where he was bound for, one of them asked:

"And where have you come from, young man?"

"From Troezen," Theseus answered simply.

The Phytalids exchanged glances.

"But the road is swarming with bandits," one of them said.

"It was, but not any more," Theseus replied.

"What do you mean?" they asked.

"I will tell you," said the hero – and he recounted everything that had happened to him on his way.

The Phytalids listened open-mouthed as the young hero

told them of his marvellous exploits. When the long tale was over, someone asked:

"Does this mean that the road to the Peloponnese is open now?"

"Open," replied Theseus. And they all gazed at the fearless young man in gratitude and admiration.

Then the Phytalids offered to purify Theseus from the blood-guilt of the murders. This they did with all the ritual which the ceremony of cleansing required. They washed him in the River Cephissus, then offered sacrifice to Gracious Zeus and the other gods. Thus all the killings were forgiven him – as, indeed, was necessary, for there was always some evil-doer under the protection of a god who might seek revenge for his death.

Purified and cleansed, Theseus dressed himself in fresh clothes, bade the Phytalids a grateful farewell and walked toward the city of Athens.

At the entrance to the city, some masons were working on the temple of Apollo. As Theseus passed by, they were putting on the roof; and when they saw the young stranger, freshly washed and wearing a long robe, which was an unusual sight in Athens, they took him for a girl and began

*...Theseus seized a wagon which was standing nearby
and tossed it right over the roof of the temple...*

to shout remarks.

Annoyed by this, and to show them just how wrong they were, Theseus seized a wagon which was standing nearby, lifted it above his head and tossed it right over the roof of the temple.

The builders were staggered by the strength of the long-robed figure and realized not only that this was no girl who stood below, but a hero fair as a god and powerful as a Titan – one whose arrival boded great things for the city.

In the meantime, the Phytalids had sent word to Aegeus, telling him that a young man was coming to see him, one who though small in years was great in soul, having wiped out all the bandits that lurked on the road linking Athens to the Peloponnese. So when the heralds announced Theseus' arrival, Aegeus ordered them to seat him by his side, at the royal table. He did this, of course, without the ghost of a suspicion that the young man was his son. Besides, he had never learned whether Aethra had actually borne a child.

Aegeus was now married to Medea. He had kept his word to her in the hope she might enable him to acquire the son he longed for. But now that he was advanced in years, it was Medea the sorceress who held the palace reins

– so tightly, indeed, that in reality she ruled the whole of Athens.

Immediately she set eyes on Theseus, Medea guessed his identity and knew at once that should the city gain an heir like this, she would cease to be the ruling power in Athens. Without a shadow of remorse, she decided to remove him from the scene. To achieve this aim she played upon her husband's fear of the Pallas clan. Now this Pallas, though the king's brother, was a deadly enemy. Seeing that Aegeus had still not begotten an heir, he wished to snatch the throne from him and later pass it to his fifty sons. Already he had made one attempt to seize power, and that having failed he had withdrawn from Athens and built the village in Attica which has been known as Pallini ever since. Nevertheless, the flame of hatred still burned strong between them, and Aegeus had never ceased to fear Pallas and his fifty sons.

Media knew all this, and out of the depths of her cunning she spun Aegeus a tale of Theseus' being a spy and a killer sent to Athens by the Pallantids.

"If you value your life," she whispered, "you must kill him. But so it will not seem that it was you who did the deed, I have poured some drops of wolfsbane in his wine. It is the deadliest poison in the world."

The guests came to take their places at the table, Theseus among them. Aegeus was troubled in his heart. What was about to happen did not please him at all. Had he any choice, though? Could he let the Pallas family take his throne, and perhaps kill him, too? So let Medea have her way, then. Yet so uneasy was the king's conscience that he could not look at Theseus – and thus of course, he saw neither his sword nor the sandals that he wore. But he invited him to sit by his side, before the cup which held the deadly poison.

The moment came for toasts of welcome to the stranger and, as was the custom, all raised their cups, including Theseus.

Medea's eyes were pinned on the young man. She could scarcely conceal her eagerness to see him drink the poisoned cup she had prepared. But Aegeus still could not bring himself to look him in the face. Theseus was puzzled by the king's attitude, and, taking it for coldness and indifference, decided to reveal his identity. And so, instead of drinking, he took out his sword and laid it on the table

...It was the sword he had hidden all those years ago,
beneath the stone at Troezen...

before his father's eyes.

Aegeus stared at the sword in amazement. It was the one he had hidden all those years ago, beneath the stone at Troezen. It was the sword of Cecrops! At once he looked down at the young man's feet and saw that he was wearing the familiar sandals, too.

"O Protector Zeus!" he cried, dashing the cup from Theseus' hand to smash upon the floor. And a moment later father and son were in each other's arms.

As they embraced, a wail of fear rang out. The cry came from Medea, who knew that all was lost. Hiding her face in her hands she darted from the table, ran out of the palace, fled from Athens and was never seen again.

No one was sorry to see her go. Overjoyed, Aegeus called a general assembly of the people, where he announced that the heroic newcomer was his son and proclaimed him heir to the throne of Athens.

A great feast followed next. The statues of the gods were decked with flowers, fires were lit at every altar and countless teams of oxen sacrificed so that all the people might celebrate the coming of this mighty hero and future king of Athens. The fame of young Theseus' deeds soon spread throughout the city, and the minstrels put them to music. For many days, no other songs were heard but those which told of the wondrous feats of Aegeus' son.

Against the Pallantids

While all the population of Athens greeted the arrival of Theseus with joy, the news came as a blow to Pallas and his sons. All their old hatred for Aegeus was rekindled, and Theseus, too, was now included.

"Who is this stranger?" they demanded in Pallini. "Where has he sprung from?"

"Aegeus has no children. How can he suddenly present us with a son, and one already grown to manhood, too?"

"It's a trick to make sure we never rule Athens!"

"That stripling never killed a bandit in his life."

"It's all fairy tales – and the celebration and feasting is just to make it go down with the people!"

"We know that game! But even if it is true, he's not going to get away with it!"

"To arms! Down with the usurper! Down with the stranger!"

"Now, while there's still time. If we delay, we'll lose all claim to the throne of Athens!"

All this the Pallantids said, and much more, too, as they laid their plans. A large army was hastily assembled and set off to strike at Athens.

But as soon as the preparations of Pallas and his sons became known, the whole of Athens rose to meet them. Aegeus placed Theseus in command of the city's forces, which quickly took up defensive positions around the city, denying all access to the enemy.

The army from Pallini had not yet been sighted when a herald came, one of their men from a nearby village. This herald, Leos, demanded speech with the commander-in-chief, and he was taken to Theseus.

"I am a friend," he said. "It will be the ruin of all Attica if the Pallantids take Athens, and so I have come to help you. They have laid a cunning plan, and unless I tell you of it, you will be defeated. Pallas and half his sons, with a small force, will attack the city from the direction of Sphettus. The other twenty-five, with the bulk of the army, will halt at Gargettus. They will make no move until the first force has retreated and your army has gone in pursuit, and then they will attack the undefended city."

Theseus' course of action was now clear. Leaving only a small force to defend the city from the direction of Sphettus, he led the rest of his army the other way, and caught the enemy unprepared at Gargettus. Bravely though the sons of Pallas fought, Theseus swept through them like a scythe, and they were utterly defeated. After this blow, the remainder of their force at Sphettus took to their heels and slunk back in shame to Pallini.

The Pallantids were furious at their defeat, and even more at Leos' treachery. Their ambitions thwarted, they vented their anger on the people of his village and forbade all further marriages between the people of Pallini and those of Hagnous, where Leos came from. Such was their hatred of his name that they would not even allow their heralds to utter the words "hear, o people," because the Greek word for people, "laos", was so close to the name of the detested Leos.

The bull of Marathon

In Athens, meanwhile, Theseus was the hero of the hour.

But he had further deeds of valour to perform.

At Marathon, a maddened bull was wreaking havoc all around. This was the bull which Heracles had brought back alive from Crete to Mycenae on Eurystheus' orders, but which that cowardly monarch had then set loose. Since then, hundreds had met their deaths, impaled on the monster's horns. Among them was the hero Androgeus, the son of Minos. To attempt to kill the beast, or bring it back alive, was sheer madness but this was what Theseus decided to do.

Aegeus, however, was unwilling to let his son set off for Marathon.

"This bull has brought more sorrows on us than you know," he told Theseus, "and I will not let you go to add to them."

"Father," said Theseus, "it will cause more sorrow still if left to live. I must go. I believe I can defeat it."

"Perhaps you must," sighed Aegeus. "Alas! What can I say? So many years I waited for a son."

But an old courtier spoke up:

"You waited for a son and you were given one worthy and brave, a true hero. You do not show a father's love by seating him on soft cushions, but by admiring his brave deeds. Who do you expect to kill the bull – or will you leave it free to bring us all to grief?"

And so Aegeus finally gave Theseus his blessing and allowed him to set off for Marathon. Filled with courage and high hopes, the young man went to find the bull and kill it.

On the road to Marathon, he met a poor old woman named Hecale, who lived all alone in a miserable hovel at the foot of Mount Pentelicon.

Theseus greeted her warmly and shared his food with her, then said where he was bound and what his mission was.

"No, my child!" Hecale cried. "You are young and handsome. Do not throw your youth away in a vain struggle with that bull!" But when she saw her words had no effect, she promised, poor though she was, to sacrifice a ram to Zeus if only she saw Theseus come back safe and sound. And as she was bidding him farewell he seemed so like a boy to her that she caressed his cheek. She would have kissed him like a son, as well, had not her face been wet with tears.

The poor old woman never made her sacrifice, for before the hero had returned she died. Theseus never forgot the kindness she had shown him, though; and later, when he became king of Athens, he went to the place where he had met Hecale and built a temple there which he named the temple of Zeus Hecaleius. He also founded the Hecalesian games, a festival in her honour. And why all this? What had Hecale had to offer Theseus? Nothing at all, if we measure kindness only in terms of material gain. But sometimes a mere tear or a soft pat on the cheek are worth far more than they seem. To his credit, Theseus saw their worth – and thus the memory of Hecale has never been forgotten. Though thousands of years have gone by since then, the place where she once lived still bears her name.

Theseus, like Heracles before him, caught the bull alive. With hands like steel pincers he seized it by the horns, bound it fast and brought it back to Athens. After dragging it in triumph through the streets of the city, he carried it up to the Acropolis, where he sacrificed it at the altar of the goddess Athena to the cheers of the assembled Athenians.

A bloody tribute

But their joy was soon forgotten, for black days were approaching, days of hopelessness and grief. And here is the reason why.

Three years before, when Theseus was still living in Troezen, a great athletic contest had been held in Athens. Among the competitors was the hero Androgeus, son of the mighty Minos, king of Crete. He took part in all the events, and in each one he came first, much to the disgust of Aegeus and all the Athenians. So much so, indeed, that Aegeus shouted out:

"If you're really such a champion, you should be able to kill the bull of Marathon as well."

Confident of yet another victory, Androgeus went straight to Marathon, but there his winning streak was ended. In the struggle with the hideous monster, the son of Minos met his death.

When the great king of Crete received the news, he vowed revenge.

"The Athenians will pay dearly for this," he swore and

immediately prepared for war.

It was not long before a vast fleet of Cretan warships appeared off Phaleron. Minos' army quickly disembarked and advanced on Athens. The Athenians, weak and unprepared, were in a desperate situation; faced by the might of all-powerful Crete, soldiers and citizens alike had no choice but to take refuge within the city walls.

Minos encircled Athens and a lengthy siege began. It was not long before hunger and sickness began to take their toll of the Athenians. In desperation, they consulted the oracle for advice – and were told that all their sufferings were a punishment sent by the gods for provoking Androgeus to go and fight the bull of Marathon. Only if they met the demands of the king of Crete would the siege be lifted.

But what Minos demanded left them horror-struck.

"You will give me your seven finest young men and your seven fairest maidens to take with me to Crete, there to be eaten by the Minotaur, and this you will do each year until nine years have passed."

The whole of Athens was plunged into mourning by this news, but they had no choice other than to obey the oracle and submit to Minos' ultimatum.

The Minotaur was a fearsome man-eating monster with a human body and the head of a bull. It lived in the Labyrinth, a building of such complexity and extent that no one who went in could ever find his way out again. And now the day was fast approaching when for the third time the Athenians would have to send seven young men and seven maidens as tribute to the Minotaur.

The day came for the victims to be chosen and Theseus still knew nothing, for Aegeus had forbidden all mention of the subject in his hearing. But the pall of gloom which hung over the city aroused the young man's suspicions. Going out into the streets, he stopped everyone he saw and tried to find out what was happening. All those he questioned just lowered their eyes and shook their heads – until an unlucky father whose child had been singled out to make the voyage to Crete could contain himself no longer and cried:

"Enough of this mockery! Why should the son of Aegeus be exempt, and only our children be eaten by the Minotaur?"

Theseus could not believe his ears. A crowd gathered,

and the young hero ordered them to tell him exactly what was afoot.

At last the truth came out.

"I shall go to Crete as well!" he shouted, "and either die with the others or free Athens from this bloody tribute once and for all!"

When Aegeus heard this he was horrified. Once again he tried to restrain his son, but in vain. He had no choice but to hide his sorrow and accept.

Theseus took his place among the seven young men.

The first thing he did was to choose two other youths from among the bravest and most strongly-built in Athens, lads who could kill a man with a single blow. He dressed these young men up as girls and substituted them for two of the maidens, whom he sent home. He then took careful precautions to make sure they would not be discovered, teaching them to walk and speak in a feminine manner and dressing their hair to make them look like girls. When everything was ready they went all together to the temple of Apollo to offer the golden-haired god the "branch of vows,"

which was an olive branch bound with white cords. And when Theseus asked the oracle which deity he should call upon for aid, he was told to seek the help and guidance of Aphrodite, goddess of love. This he later did, as we shall see.

The hour arrived for the young people to set sail for Crete. Theseus tried to give them courage. He told the young men and the maidens not to be afraid, for this time none of them would come to harm. He gave the same message of hope to the Athenians, and tried to reassure the young people's parents. Nothing could assuage their grief, however, for none believed that their children could be saved. Indeed, many of them were sadder still at the thought that now Theseus, too, the pride and hope of Athens, was doomed to lose his life.

King Aegeus was torn between despair and the hope Theseus gave him of a miracle. Thus, although their ship was to voyage to Crete as it had done each time before, with the black sail of catastrophe and death, he gave his son a white one, too, to hoist on the return journey, if, indeed, they were destined to come back alive.

The youths and maidens went on board their ship, which,

strange though it may seem, was not Athenian. The city which was one day to become a mighty naval power did not yet have one ship of its own, nor a single man who knew the mysteries of the sea. But an experienced seafarer from the islands, Phaeax by name, offered to take them to Crete in his ship. And luckily he did, for otherwise they would have had to use a Cretan vessel, these being the only ones readily available in those times. This would have been a serious obstacle to Theseus' plan, which was not only to kill the Minotaur, but bring the whole group safely back to Athens.

When they landed in Crete they found Minos waiting for them on the shore. The young people disembarked and Minos looked them over carefully, one by one. Theseus was worried about the two young men he had dressed as girls, but so perfect was their disguise that Minos suspected nothing. Something else caught his eye, however, the lovely Eriboea, and being a man used to taking just what he wanted, without regard for others' wishes, he stretched out his hand and began to fondle her. Immediately, Theseus stepped between them.

"We came here to be killed – not dishonoured!" he said with dignity.

"Who are you to tell me what to do?" snarled Minos. "You forget I am the king of mighty Crete! And if that does not suffice, know that I am the son of Zeus as well – for it seems you do not know it!"

Then, raising his eyes to the heavens, he lifted up his arms and shouted: "O father Zeus, show them who I am!"

Hardly had he spoken when a flash of lightning streaked across a cloudless sky, proof that Zeus had recognised his son.

Theseus was startled but, as ever, not dismayed.

"If such things are of importance to you," he remarked, "then I must inform you that I, too, am of divine birth. My father is Poseidon, ruler of the seas."

Minos did not believe him.

"If you are Poseidon's son," he sneered, "you should be able to bring this back to me." And with these words he pulled off his ring and flung it far into the depths of the sea.

Immediately, Theseus dived into the water and was lost to sight beneath its surface.

*...Poseidon was delighted to see Theseus, and ordered
Triton to go in search of the ring...*

A long time passed, but he did not reappear.

All those on the shore were convinced he had been drowned, and Minos added:

"A pity! That makes one less for the Minotaur to eat."

But Ariadne, Minos' daughter, who stood nearby, could hardly keep her sobs back, and secretly wiped the tears from her eyes. She had noticed Theseus from the moment he came ashore, and his bravery had stirred her heart. A passionate love had kindled there, fired by the arrow Aphrodite's winged son Eros had shot into her heartstrings; now she was torn by grief at the loss of the bold young man.

Yet Theseus was anything but lost. The moment he dived into the water, dolphins had led him swiftly to the palace of the sea god, earth-shaker Poseidon, who was the brother of Zeus and no less in power than he who wields the lightning.

The ruler of the waves sat on a majestic throne fashioned from a vast sea shell. At his side sat the lovely Amphitrite, his wife, while nearby stood Triton and other deities of the ocean.

Poseidon was delighted to see Theseus, and as soon as

he learned why he had come to his watery kingdom, he ordered Triton to go in search of the ring.

It was not long before the sea god returned, accompanied by a host of Nereids. One of these was holding the ring, which she gave to Theseus. Then Amphitrite placed a golden circlet on his hair while Poseidon, who realized that Theseus should delay no longer, ordered Triton and the Nereids to lead him back to shore.

Theseus emerged from the sea just as the watchers on the land were leaving. Suddenly, one of them shouted:

"Theseus! Theseus has returned!"

Against the Minotaur

When Minos saw him, he hardly dared believe his eyes. Not only had Theseus not drowned, but he wore on his brow a garland of leaves worked in solid gold. His surprise was even greater when the young man approached and handed him back the ring he had flung into the sea. Convinced now that Theseus was no common mortal, he feared him. And for this reason he said to his followers:

"The Minotaur must devour him first!"

Ariadne listened to her father's words in horror. She was moved to pity for all these young men and women, but when she heard Theseus' name, it was as if a knife had been turned inside her.

Minos ordered all the Athenians to be thrown into prison, but for Theseus to be kept apart.

"And tomorrow morning you will take him to the Labyrinth to be eaten by the Minotaur," he added.

Ariadne could no longer contain her anguish.

"O great goddess of love," she whispered, "what have I done to make you plant this arrow in my heart?" And she leaned her head upon the shoulder of her sister Phaedra so that none might see her tears. Phaedra turned and gave her an anxious look.

"Why are you crying so?" she asked. "They are not the first ones to be eaten by the Minotaur, nor will they be the last."

Ariadne drew her sister aside.

"Help me, Phaedra," she implored, "or I shall die. We must save that young man!" And with her eyes she pointed out Theseus.

"Are you mad, Ariadne?" came the shocked reply. "Our

father will kill us both. Do you not know that he cares more about the Minotaur than us?"

"Help me, Phaedra!" Ariadne begged. "Tell me what I can do to save him."

"I fear there is nothing to be done," her sister said. "Not even Daedalus could find a way to save him."

"Daedalus!" cried Ariadne, and a gleam of hope lit up her eyes. Leaving Phaedra standing there, she ran to the workshop of the great inventor.

Daedalus was the Athenian who had built the Labyrinth. Not only was he a great architect and artist, too, but the most inventive man the world had ever known. As soon as he saw Minos' daughter standing in the doorway, he called out:

"Ariadne, you have come at just the right moment!"

"I need your help, wise teacher," Ariadne said.

"And I need yours," was his reply. "We must save the young people of Athens, and you are the only one who can help me."

When Ariadne heard these words, she was overcome with joy.

"That is why I came to you," she sobbed.

"Then listen to me," said Daedalus. "Among them is Theseus, the son of Aegeus. Theseus is a great hero who has killed robbers, evil-doers and monsters, and I believe that he can kill the Minotaur as well. The greatest difficulty does not lie there, but in finding his way out of the Labyrinth. I constructed it myself, on Minos' orders, but I never dreamed it would become the dwelling place of a monster. The Labyrinth is of very strange construction. Its corridors, its galleries, its staircases and its doors are so devised that while it is easy to go in and find your way to the centre, it is utterly impossible to find your way out again."

"Wise Daedalus," begged Ariadne, "find me a way."

"I have found the way already," Daedalus reassured her. "But someone must meet Theseus in secret and speak with him. You are the only person I can think of. Take this spool of thread with you. Find a means to give it to him without being seen, and tell him to tie one end near the entrance and then move inwards, unwinding the spool as he goes."

"I understand!" cried Ariadne. "It's the perfect way!"

"Yes," replied Daedalus. "By winding the thread back afterwards he will find the entrance once again and save his life. As for the rest of what must be done, I have confidence in Theseus. All I fear is that your father's suspicions may finally fall on you. He would even kill you for it if they did."

"I know," said Ariadne, "and for that reason I shall flee with Theseus – and if he wants to share his life with me. O Daedalus, wise teacher, if only you knew how much I owe you!"

"Ah, Ariadne," Daedalus replied, "if you but knew how much I owe to you as well! I am Athenian, and my heart bleeds for my city; it bleeds, too, for its young folk who are sacrificed. There is another reason for my grief, as well: I live in exile, and while my dream is to use my talents for my fellow men, I end up raising palaces for monsters. If Theseus is saved, then maybe I, too, will be able to return to the land which gave me birth, there to build and create lovely things for all those who love beauty. But this is no time for words. Go quickly, now, and do what you must."

"I shall fly, dear Daedalus. Your words have given me wings," cried Ariadne. "Theseus shall be saved, and all the young people of Athens along with him."

With the spool of thread hidden under her arm, Ariadne

ran to find Theseus and greeted him.

"I am the daughter of king Minos, and strange though it may seem to you I do not want to see you killed. If you died, I would want to die as well."

Theseus was startled by her words. Then suddenly he remembered he had sought the aid of Aphrodite, and everything was clear. He looked at Ariadne and she seemed as lovely as a goddess. He admired her for her courage, he was blinded by her beauty, and he, too, fell in love upon the instant.

"I did not come here to die," he answered, "but to kill the Minotaur."

"That is a thing no man can do," said Ariadne. "Yet something tells me that you will succeed. But even so, you will never see the light of day again unaided, for no one who enters the Labyrinth can ever find the way to leave it. That is why I have come in search of you. Take this spool of thread. When you enter the Labyrinth, tie the end of it near the entrance and as you go further in, unwind the spool. It is the only way to save yourself from getting lost. On your return, wind up the thread once more, and you will find the door. Once you are safely outside, there is only one thing that I beg of you: do not leave me in Crete, for my father could kill me for what I have done. You must take me away with you – and if you wish to make me yours, I shall be the happiest woman in the world."

The hero was delighted. "My thanks to you, mighty goddess," he said when Ariadne had left him; and in the morning, when they put him in the Labyrinth, he tied one end of the thread to the entrance, unwinding the spool as he went forward. The way inside the Labyrinth was confusing beyond belief. Sometimes it went this way, sometimes that; sometimes it went back on itself, sometimes straight forward; sometimes it went left and sometimes right; sometimes it led him upwards and sometimes down. He had been walking in this dizzying fashion for many hours when suddenly, when he least expected it, he found himself face to face with the Minotaur.

The battle with the monster began at once. The hideous beast lowered its horns and charged at Theseus. But the young hero dodged nimbly to one side and plunged his sword in the creature's flanks. The blow had but little effect upon the Minotaur, however; it turned and lunged again and again, though never quickly enough to prevent Theseus from stepping aside unharmed. In the end, unable to keep up the pace, his opponent paused for breath. This was the moment Theseus had been waiting for. Seizing the Minotaur by the horns, he hurled it to the ground with unbelievable strength and plunged his sword into its breast. The monster of the Labyrinth would never claim another victim.

The hero gazed down at the dead Minotaur, wiped the sweat from his forehead and said:

"Now all that remains is to find the way out."

Winding the thread back on the spool, he began the return journey. Luckily for him, he had the spool. For while his instinct told him that he should turn one way, the thread led him the other; and while something told him that this way was right, the growing spool he held told him in fact another direction was correct. He could not understand why the thread was leading him through such an unbelievable maze of passages and he went on in growing bewilderment, until at last, when the spool had become a heavy ball, he found himself before the entrance once again.

"Without that thread I would have been lost," he told himself. "Ariadne saved me!"

...The battle with the monster began at once...

And there in the doorway was the lovely maiden, waiting for him. She was alone. Once Theseus had entered the Labyrinth, king Minos had thought it quite unnecessary to place guards at the entrance.

With tears of joy streaming down her face, Ariadne fell into Theseus' arms. Unable to find words to thank her, he silently gave back the ball of thread. And ever since, "Ariadne's thread" has been a symbol to the Greeks which represents the way out of a difficult situation.

The voyage home

There was no time to be lost. Taking Ariadne by the hand, Theseus set off in search of the others. He soon found the place where they were kept, but this time it was guarded. Ariadne was afraid.

"Do not be frightened," Theseus reassured her. "All will be well." And he whistled three times.

When the young people heard his signal, they jumped up from the floor of their prison, charged all together at the door and burst it open. The guards came running up and saw two maidens about to leave the cell. They went to push them back inside – and got two punches for their pains that laid them flat on their backs. The other guards came rushing in and were given a dose of the same medicine – for these two maidens were not girls at all, but the two strong youths who were dressed in women's clothes. A moment later, Theseus arrived, sword in hand, but there was no need for him to do anything. All resistance had been crushed. Without a moment's delay they set off for the sea shore.

At this time of the day there was not a soul in sight. The Cretan vessels were all drawn up on land, and only their own ship floated on the water.

"Before we go aboard," cried Theseus, "come and stove in the hulls of Minos' fleet; for if they come in pursuit of us, we may be overtaken."

They quickly holed each Cretan ship below the waterline, then went on board their own vessel and, happier than words can tell, set sail for Athens.

When Minos learned of what had happened, he was wild with rage – and he had good reason to be furious: not only had Theseus killed the Minotaur and they had all escaped; not only had his daughter Ariadne helped them; but worse still, she had run off with them, too.

"Wherever they go, I shall catch them!" he vowed, immediately ordering his ships to be launched in pursuit.

But his ships were full of holes, and as soon as they reached the open sea, they all went to the bottom.

Minos returned to his palace in despair.

"To think that Ariadne is to blame for all this!" he told himself. In the end, however, since there was nothing he could do about it, he thought the matter over and said:

"What could I do about it, anyway? It was the will of the gods. And then, she is my daughter, after all. Let's hope it all works out for her good. As for Theseus, well, I must admit he is no mere adventurer, but the son of Poseidon." Then, content with his reasoning, he let the matter rest.

Theseus' ship sailed northwards till it reached the isle of Naxos, where they had to put ashore to spend the night. As they were sleeping on the beach, Dionysus the god of wine appeared to Theseus and said:

"Arise at once and sail away; leave Ariadne on the shore, for this is the will of Zeus, ruler of gods and men."

Filled with sorrow, but unable to ignore the god's command, Theseus roused his comrades. Once he had told them the message that had come to him in his sleep, they all agreed to leave immediately.

And so they went on board their ship once more and set sail for Athens, leaving Ariadne fast asleep on the sand.

When the girl awoke and saw that they were gone, she wept bitter tears.

"How could he be so ungrateful?" she sobbed.

At that moment, Dionysus appeared.

"There is no ingratitude," he told her, "and Theseus is not to blame. It was I who ordered him to sail away and leave you here alone upon the shore. For it is the will of mighty Zeus that you become my wife."

Thus Ariadne, daughter of Minos, was wedded to the god Dionysus.

In Athens, meanwhile, king Aegeus had lived in anguish since the moment Theseus and the other young people had left. Not one night could he get a wink of sleep, so in the end he decided to move down to Cape Sounion. There he sat on a tall rock, high above the sea, and patiently scanned the horizon, hoping to see Theseus' ship appear, bearing the white sail which would lift the burden that weighed upon his heart.

But instead, a tiny dark speck came into view above the edge of the horizon. Aegeus did not have the courage to believe this was the black sail of the ship he had been waiting for. But the speck grew larger and larger until he saw beyond all trace of doubt that it was indeed the sad colour of catastrophe and death. What he had feared so much had come to pass. His son had been eaten by the Minotaur!

"Luckless old man," he seemed to hear a voice saying to him, "you longed for a son to bring you joy and ease. You gained the son you so much wanted, but what did it bring you? Grief and ruin!"

Like a lost soul, Aegeus cast one last look at that black sail which had broken his heart and, unable to bear his sufferings any longer, threw himself from the high rock down into the foaming waves below.

For Theseus, alas, what with his joy at their escape, and what with the perils and alarms he and his companions had been through, had completely forgotten that he should have hoisted the white sail in place of the black. And so, while Aegeus was sinking beneath the waves, his son continued his carefree voyage to Athens, completely unaware that anything was amiss.

...Aegeus threw himself from the high rock down into the foaming waves below...

As soon as Theseus and his comrades came ashore, at
Phaleron, he ordered a herald to run to Athens with all
speed, to bring the good news to the people of the city and
delight his father's heart. He and the others remained behind to make the sacrifices which were owed to the gods,
and to offer their thanks for bringing them all home safe
and victorious.

The sacrifices had been completed when they saw the
herald returning with a crowd of Athenians, who approached shouting: "Elelev! Iou! Iou!"

The voyagers could make nothing of these cries, for
while "Elelev!" was a shout of joy, "Iou" meant exactly
the opposite.

All too soon they learned the awful meaning of those
cries, and Theseus wept tears of remorse for his unforgiv-
able forgetfulness which had led Aegeus to throw away
his life. His comrades wept as inconsolably as he for the
loss of their king; yet this was not a time for tears alone,
but also for great joy. And so the return of Theseus to Athens became a triumphal march. At its head strode the son
of Aegeus, while behind him came the two strong youths
who had been dressed as maidens, followed by all the other

young men and women.

With the same cries of mingled grief and rejoicing, the whole of Athens welcomed Theseus and his companions – some strewing olive branches in their path, and others crowning them with garlands from which white ribbons hung, an honour usually paid only to the statues of the gods.

The people's relief at the great victory soon dispelled their sorrow at Aegeus' death. Not only had the Minotaur been killed, but more important still, the young voyagers had all returned safe and well. From now on, too, Athens would have Theseus for its king, the hero who had saved their children's lives. But so that the memory of Aegeus should never be forgotten, they renamed the sea which had swallowed up that luckless father, and called it the Aegean.

Theseus, king of Athens

Theseus ruled Athens wisely and with love, taking the side of the poor and weak as none had done before him. He hated tyranny, and it is said that it was he who first taught the people to take their own decisions regarding the affairs of their city. His concern for his fellow men extended not only to the Athenians, but to all the folk of Attica. Clamping down on the great landowners who had exploited the villagers for so long and ruled like petty kings, he united all the towns and villages of Attica under one government. This "State of the Athenians" made all the people of the region citizens of Athens. It is from this period that the plural "s" on Athens dates, showing that one state was formed by uniting the city with all the other towns of Attica. In the same way, the great "Festival of the Athenians," as it was called till then, became the "Panathenian Festival" since all the inhabitants of Attica now took part in it.

Theseus placed great importance on athletics, too. Just as Heracles had started the Olympic Games in honour of his father, Olympian Zeus, so Theseus founded the Isthmian Games, another great sporting and artistic contest which was held every three years at the Isthmus of Corinth, in honour of the sea god Poseidon, who was said to be Theseus' father.

The new king of Athens was a peace-loving man as well. During his reign he made no wars on other races, although he continued to love feats of daring and acts of heroism. This is why he joined Jason and the Argonauts in the search for the Golden Fleece, and was among the many heroes who hunted down the Calydonian Boar. Last of all, he accompanied Heracles on his campaign in the land of the Amazons.

It was for this reason that the Athenians said so proudly that nothing could be done without Theseus, and even called him another Heracles – for when he went with that great hero to the country of the Amazons to bring back Hippolyta's belt, the two fought side by side, and Theseus showed once more the heroism and self-sacrifice which made him worthy of the comparison.

In that battle, Theseus made a prisoner of Antiope, one of the three queens of the Amazons, and brought her back with him to Athens. He fell in love with his proud captive, and made her not his slave, but his wife. By him she bore a son, Hippolytus, a pure and handsome youth who dedicated his life to the goddess Artemis.

But while Antiope was in fact happily married to Theseus, her fellow Amazons in their distant homeland were tortured by the thought that she, their queen, was suf-

fering all the indignities of slavery in the palace of the king of Athens. And so they decided to launch a campaign against the city and set her free. They sailed up in their ships, landed in Attica, and struck at the city. These blood-thirsty women were so formidable that all the armies in the world stood in fear of them. Besides, their blow had fallen upon Athens without any warning. Before the wild charge of the Amazons, who swept in on horseback sowing death and destruction all around them, the Athenians had no hope of fighting back, and fled up to the Acropolis

to find refuge within its walls. There Theseus at last or-
ganised a successful defence and then prepared for the
counter-attack. Antiope, whose love for her husband was
as strong as ever, never imagined for a moment that the
Amazons had in fact launched this campaign out of love
for her. On the contrary, she, like Theseus, believed their
attack to be prompted by revenge and greed. And so she
stood firm by her husband's side, and fought along with
him.

At last the day of the decisive battle came. It was a fearsome, bloody struggle. The Athenians fought desperately, in the belief that they were defending their very homeland and the altars of their gods, while the Amazons attacked with redoubled ferocity to free the queen they all believed to be an unhappy slave. Violently as the fighting raged, however, neither side could gain the upper hand.

Suddenly the Amazons saw a fair young horseman in shining armour spur forward from the ranks and urge the Athenians on with superb and unflinching courage. They flung themselves upon him in a swarm, and savage fighting broke out all around, until an arrow fired by the Amazon Molpadia toppled the handsome warrior from his saddle, dead. The Amazons ran with fierce cries to seize the corpse and humble the Athenians still further. Renewed fighting had broken out over the body when suddenly one of them cried:

"Lay down your arms! It is Antiope we have killed!"

As if by magic, the battle came to a halt, and the two opposing armies stood united in their grief over the brave Antiope, once a queen of the Amazons and then the queen of Athens.

She was buried amid universal mourning, and soon afterwards the Amazons set sail for their distant homeland, their hearts heavy with remorse at their unjust invasion and its tragic consequences.

Theseus, too, was inconsolable, and mourned Antiope for many days to come. But in the end time softened his pain, for the demands of the living were ever present and his duties as ruler of Athens could not be neglected. In the meantime, that great enemy of the Athenians, king Minos, had died and been succeeded on the throne of Crete by his son Deucalion, a man very different from his father, and one who believed that nothing could come of cherishing old hatreds. Besides, Athens under Theseus was no longer a weak and defenceless city, but a power to be reckoned with.

For his part, Theseus saw no purpose in keeping old wounds open for the sake of hating, and he offered Deucalion both friendship and alliance. Deucalion accepted, and, to bind their new alliance firmer still, he proposed that Theseus should take his sister Phaedra for his wife, a suggestion which the Athenian king happily agreed to. Thus a great bond of common interest was sealed between Athens and the island of Crete.

From his marriage with Phaedra, Theseus had two sons, one of whom, Demophon, later became king of Athens. But his union with the daughter of Minos did not bring Theseus good fortune. Instead of being a loving wife and queen to him, Phaedra laid false charges against Hippolytus, the son Antiope had borne him, and thus caused a tragedy which resulted in the death of Hippolytus and her own suicide. This unhappy tale moved the Athenians deeply, and Euripides' immortal tragedy "Hippolytus" still stirs men's hearts today as it did in those distant years.

Later, Theseus sealed another, deeper, bond of friendship, this time with Peirithous, king of the Lapiths, a brave tribe who lived in Thessaly.

Peirithous was a fearless warrior and hero who made his acquaintance with Theseus in a rather strange way. Hearing of the Athenian's numerous bold achievements, he was envious of his fame and obsessed by the idea that this Theseus was overshadowing his own glory. And so Peirithous determined to humble him, to show the world which of the two was the greater man.

With this aim in mind, he went to Marathon and seized a herd of Theseus' finest oxen, telling the terrified herdsmen:

"Go and tell your king that his oxen were taken by Peirithous, the bravest man on earth. I challenge him to come and get them back from me – if he dares!"

This was a mortal insult to Theseus, who set off in search of the thief at once – not so much to retrieve his oxen as to wipe clean this slur on his reputation.

The two heroes caught sight of each other just beyond Marathon. When Theseus spotted Peirithous from afar, and Peirithous saw Theseus, the two of them advanced with grim determination, their pace steady and their eyes burning with cold rage. Each had but a single thought in mind: to kill his opponent or to die in the attempt.

When they drew near, both stopped and placed their hands upon their sword-hilts to signal they were ready for the duel. But in that moment, neither could but admire the other for his courage and good looks and the splendid figure that he cut as he stood there in his shining armour. It seemed to each of them that he was looking on a god.

Eventually, both drew their swords to strike; but then, in mid-blow, their arms froze and something quite unexpected happened. Throwing their swords aside, they stood and gazed in admiration at each other. But only for a moment; then their looks grew dark once more and they lunged in furious attack. But yet again, they could not find it in their hearts to strike each other, and throwing wide their arms, they embraced and kissed. From this moment on they swore eternal friendship, sealing the bond with an exchange of swords.

Now Theseus and Peirithous were friends till death, and the links between them were forged firmer still when Theseus helped Peirithous to defeat the fearsome Centaurs who tried to snatch his lovely bride Deidameia from him in the middle of their wedding ceremony.

In the battle with these strange horse-like creatures, Theseus showed his skill and courage yet again. With the exception of wise old Cheiron, the Centaurs were a savage and formidable race who wreaked destruction throughout Greece. They were dreaded by kings, heroes and common folk alike, and everybody treated them with respect lest they suffer worse still at their hands. Theseus was the first man to win a victory over them, and under his leadership the Centaurs, invincible till now, met with such a crushing defeat that they never again spread terror in that region.

Later, Heracles wiped out the few that still remained, and so the earth was troubled by their presence no longer and the hills and valleys at last found their peace.

Here the story of Theseus might be drawn to its close – indeed, most authors end it at this point. From now on there are no more wondrous feats; and those who wish to leave their readers with a good impression of the mighty hero may have their point. But it would be a disservice to mythology not to tell the whole story and say merely that "they all lived happily ever after," when in fact the end was not like that at all.

The downfall

So let us go on with the tale, and if it does not close to Theseus' credit, at least some lesson may be drawn from it more valuable than any "happy" ending.

Unluckily for both of them, no good at all came out of the friendship between Theseus and Peirithous.

Soon after the battle with the savage Centaurs, Peirithous' wife died, and since Theseus' wife Phaedra had already killed herself, the two of them decided to remarry.

So each of them could win the wife he had set his heart on, they promised to help each other all the way.

This may not have seemed a bad idea, yet bad it was, for what each set his heart on was beyond all reason.

It is truly sad for such men to end up losing all sense of what is right – yet it happens often enough. Just as such madness can be found in mythology, we find it in real life, too, which only goes to show how close are fact and myth in spirit, for all the latter's flights of fancy. And while many men do wild things in their youth, yet grow up to become steady and responsible, it was exactly the opposite in the case of the two friends.

So when, at the age of fifty, Theseus decided to remarry, he chose none other than the fair Helen, daughter of Zeus and Leda, a maiden barely twelve years old! With such a difference in their ages, he dared not ask her hand in marriage, but decided to abduct her.

As they had agreed, he went to Peirithous and said:

"Help me now, and when the time comes, I will help you, too, to take the woman of your dreams."

Peirithous kept his word and the two of them went to Sparta and kidnapped Helen. They snatched her from among her friends, as she was dancing in the temple of Artemis. Hastily carrying her back to Attica, they concealed her in the village of Aphidnae, where Theseus' mother Aethra was now living. What could the poor old woman do but agree to guard young Helen and to keep her company while Theseus was away? And so the kidnapping itself was accomplished without much difficulty. It was later that difficulties were to arise – and they would prove disastrous.

But if Theseus' choice was a mad one, Peirithous' was ten times so. First of all, he chose to take a goddess for his wife; secondly, this goddess was already married, and third – and worst of all for him – her husband, too, was a god, and one whose very name men feared to utter. But Peirithous ignored all this. All that concerned him was how to put the matter to Theseus. In the end, he found a way.

"Who took fair Helen for his bride?" he asked.

"The daughter of Zeus, you mean!" said Theseus proudly.

"You are become the equal of the gods – but I?"

"What do you mean, 'but I'?" came Theseus' retort. "Did we not say: 'choose who you will'? There's two of us to do the job, both fearless, and so strong no man's a match for us. Do you still hesitate?"

"Well done, Theseus!" cried Peirithous. "You're a man after my own heart. You know I'd go down to the kingdom of the dead for you."

"And I would go to Tartarus itself for your sake," said Theseus.

"Now that's what I call friendship!" Peirithous laughed. "And here I was wondering how to put it to you. Yes, it's the kingdom of the dead I had in mind. I want Persephone, the wife of Pluto!"

When Theseus heard this, his mouth fell open. But what could he say? He had given his word again and again, and now he could not go back on it. Besides, how could he let his fear show, when Peirithous had set his mind on such a daring feat? And so, without delay, the two friends put the mad scheme into action.

From a deep gorge near Colonus, they descended to the kingdom of the underworld. At first, everything went well. They tricked the boatman Charon and he ferried them across the sacred underground river men call the Styx; next they passed without difficulty through the gates of Hades, which are guarded by the hideous dog Cerberus, and then they cautiously advanced on the palace of Pluto, taking great care not to be observed by the fearsome king of the dead.

Their plan was to seize Persephone without his knowing, but, being a god, Pluto knew exactly what was going on, and suddenly appeared before them.

"What do you two living creatures want down here in Hades?" he demanded, with a cool air that showed little of the rage he felt inside him.

The two friends gaped at him in horror. They didn't have the first idea what to answer. After an awkward pause, Peirithous found his tongue and stammered:

"Well, er, you see, we're having a party at my palace, and we were wondering – if you didn't have any objection, of course – whether you would let Persephone come and honour us with her presence."

"I see. Just Persephone – not me?" asked Pluto, beginning to enjoy himself with this foolish pair.

"Oh, yes, yes; you too, of course!" they blurted in confusion.

"These two aren't half as clever as they think," said Pluto to himself; and still hiding his anger he said:

"Listen, such feasts and merrymaking are not for the likes of me – but take Persephone by all means. She could do with a little fun. Just sit down on these chairs while I go and call her." And he showed them to two stone seats which stood at the entrance to his palace.

"Well done, old friend," said Theseus, once Pluto was out of earshot; and pleased that everything had gone off so smoothly, he sat down on the chair.

"Pluto will never get over it when he finds out how we've pulled the wool over his eyes," chuckled Peirithous, sitting down as well.

Then an expression of alarm appeared on Theseus' face. "Don't laugh too soon," he muttered, "I think I'm stuck to the chair!"

"What did you say?" cried Peirithous and tried to get to his feet. But he couldn't. "I'm stuck, too!" he groaned in horror.

They tried once more to free themselves, but it was impossible. They heaved with all their strength, but nothing happened. Their behinds and the stone seats had become one single solid mass, and there was no way they could get themselves unstuck. They waited in vain for Pluto to come

..."What do you two living creatures want down here in
Hades?"...

back and free them, still trying to convince themselves that something else had befallen them, and not the just punishment which their insolence deserved. In the end it was not Pluto and Persephone who came, but two great snakes, which wound themselves about their legs and bound them even more firmly to the chairs. At last they realized how rash and foolhardy they had been – but now it was too late. With all their pride and overconfidence completely knocked out of them, they looked at one another in despair. And the expression on their faces was enough to make one weep for them.

"Forgive me, Theseus," muttered Peirithous, his head bent low with shame.

"Why ask forgiveness," answered Theseus, "I was to blame as well. Thanks to our friendship, we joined forces to become stronger, but instead of using that strength for noble ends, look what we did: we came to carry off a married woman – and one married to a god, at that! If ever anyone deserved to be punished, it was us!"

The two friends remained there for a long time, until Heracles came to Hades to take Cerberus up to earth. Seeing them sitting there stuck to the stone chairs he took pity on them. With a great heave, he pulled Theseus free. But Peirithous would not come unstuck. The mighty hero tried again, tugging with even greater strength, but although his efforts caused an earthquake, Peirithous remained as firmly fixed as ever. Now Heracles knew that the gods did not wish Theseus' friend to be set free; and so he left Peirithous there, never to return to earth again.

Not that anything pleasant was awaiting Theseus, either, when he got back up to Athens after all this time.

First of all, the kidnapping of Zeus' daughter, the fair Helen, had not been without consequences. Helen had two brothers, Castor and Polydeuces, who were famous for their strength and daring. When they heard of their sister's fate and who was responsible, they roused the Spartans and swept into Attica with a huge army. In the absence of Theseus, they overcame the resistance of the Athenians and looted their city. But as for Helen, she was nowhere to be found. Castor and Polydeuces would not have left stone upon stone in Athens – or in the whole of Attica, for that matter – had a man called Academus not had the good sense to tell them where their sister was concealed. Going to Aphidnae, they found young Helen and set her free, but when they left they took Theseus' mother Aethra with them as a slave. Old though she was, it was she who paid for the follies of her son.

At Argos, Helen gave birth to a daughter who was named Iphigeneia. Her brothers gave this child of Theseus to be taken care of by her elder sister, Clytemnestra.

Clytemnestra and her husband Agamemnon, king of Mycenae, brought Iphigenia up as if she were their own child, and ever afterwards it was believed, that this girl, who was later sacrificed so that the Greek ships might have a fair wind when they set sail for the Trojan war, was really a princess of Mycenae.

But Castor and Polydeuces struck Aethra's son an even harsher blow. On leaving Attica, they appointed Menestheus, one of Theseus' cousins, as king of Athens. And so, when the hero returned, he found his place taken by another. He demanded his throne back, but Menestheus, who had no wish to give up his new title, insisted that the people should decide. Menestheus made clever use of the fact that it was Theseus who had been the cause of the war with the Spartans. He charged him with disappearing and leaving his people undefended and maintained that it was his desertion that had cost Athens such terrible destruction and so much blood.

Menestheus' arguments won the day. The Athenians, who had once loved Theseus so deeply, no longer wanted even to set eyes on him, and many of them said that if a leader wished to be worthy of his people's love until the end, then he must stay with them until the end, as well. Thus Theseus was rejected once and for all by the city he had served so brilliantly and which had praised and honoured him so highly when he was its king. In bitter despair, he took the road of exile, a shattered man. Release was all he wanted now, and only death could bring it. But even a hero's death was not destined to be granted him. Theseus' wanderings eventually brought him to Scyros, where he had some land. This property, however, had been usurped by Lycomedes, the cunning king of the island. He raised no objections about giving it back to Theseus and even took him for a walk on the pretext of pointing out its boundaries. Leading the hero to a high rock to get a better view, he gave a sudden push and sent him tumbling from its edge. Such was the inglorious fate of the greatest king and hero Athens had ever known.

Although Theseus had made grave mistakes in the last years of his life, this does not mean that all the good he did should count for nothing. For as with all men, what finally weighs most is some deed of heroism or self-sacrifice, that generosity of spirit which gives a ruler stature in the people's eyes. And Theseus served his people well, accomplished much that was brilliant and noble and became a leader who was truly great. Although there was a time when the Athenians rejected him, it did not last for long.

When Menestheus was killed in the Trojan war and Theseus' son Demophon became king of Athens in his place, the people of the city soon began to recall what splendid deeds the mighty hero had once done in their name and forgave him if at last he had unintentionally done them harm.

Demophon honoured his father not only by restoring his good name, but in performing acts of valour of his own. He won glory fighting under the walls of Troy and helped the sons of Heracles when Eurystheus tried to destroy them after their father died. Aided by Demophon, the Heraclids defeated Eurystheus and the loud-mouthed, cowardly king of Mycenae met the death which he deserved.

The Athenians loved Demophon for all his works, but especially because it was he that rescued the glorious deeds of Theseus from oblivion, thus winning him more praise than he had enjoyed within his lifetime.

The years rolled by, and then the centuries, but unlike most old things, the memory of Theseus was not forgotten. On the contrary, as Athens grew in power and renown, so did the veneration of its citizens for the man they now recognised as the greatest of their kings. Later, when Athens preserved the freedom of all the Greeks from the invading Persians and became the centre of power and culture for the whole country, the worship of Theseus spread even wider. For Theseus was now not only the hero of Athens, he was its very symbol.

And so, in the time of Cimon, five centuries before Christ, the Athenians decided to find the bones of Theseus and bring them back to his city. On asking the oracle at Delphi where they might be found, they were told to search on Scyros. Cimon himself made the journey, and there an eagle, driving its beak into the ground, showed him the spot where the hero lay buried. Cimon dug there, and found the skeleton of a tall and well-built man. Beside it lay the bronze tip of a lance, and Theseus' sword. Or so the story goes.

When the remains were carried back to Athens, it seemed as if the city were welcoming the hero-king himself, as if he were returning from his last, most brilliant feat of valour. With cries of "Elelev, Iou, Iou!" recalling his voyage back from Crete, and with grand processions and sacrifices to the gods, the Athenians buried Theseus in the centre of the city, in a spot where the weak and the cast-out had their refuge, among those he had done so much to help during his lifetime. Above his grave, a splendid monument was later built. Men called it the Theseion, and the finest sculptors and painters of the age adorned it with scenes recalling the glorious deeds of Athens' best and most beloved hero. And centuries later, when the emperor Hadrian built a new settlement adjoining Athens, he had inscribed above its gateway, on the side nearest the old city: "Here is Athens, the city of Theseus".

AEACUS AND PELEUS

Aeacus the just

Aeacus, son of Zeus by Aegina, the lovely daughter of the river-god Asopus, was founder of a line that numbered among its ranks such renowned heroes as Achilles, the greatest war-leader of all Greece. Yet how Aeacus himself came to be born is a story in itself.

When Zeus first saw Aegina, on a shady river bank, he was dazzled by her beauty and, in his usual high-handed manner, he carried the girl off without even letting her parents know. This time, however, he ran into unexpected trouble with her father, who moved heaven and earth to find his daughter and get her back again. Learning from Sisyphus who had snatched the girl away from him, and where she might be found, Asopus hastened to a forest outside Corinth, where he caught Zeus and Aegina together. In his fury he did not hesitate to attack the god whose power all other deities and mortals trembled at. So savagely did Asopus bear down on him that for the first time in his life Zeus was afraid. Taken by surprise, without a single thunder-bolt to fight back with, he seized Aegina by the hand; and then a scene unfolded such as the world had never yet set eyes on: almighty Zeus in flight, pursued by Asopus, a god who till that moment not a soul had reckoned to be either strong or brave.

He eventually found a hiding place in the thick undergrowth, but Asopus was searching everywhere and would soon have stumbled upon Zeus had he not turned himself and Aegina into a rock. As it was, the river god walked straight past them without suspecting anything, and as soon as he was out of sight Zeus seized the girl once more and set off for Olympus. But Asopus picked up his trail again, and followed him to the foothills of the mountain. There, however, the tables were turned – for now Zeus was safe behind his towering ramparts and he had his thunderbolts to hand. Furious that such an insignificant god had so humiliated him, he launched a pitiless barrage of lightning at poor Asopus, who was now transformed from avenger into victim. Only by the skin of his teeth did he make it back to Corinth, where he dived into a well to hide. Unable to flush out his quarry, Zeus wreaked his anger on the river that bears his name. If ever you should find yourself near the river Asopus, take a walk along its banks. There you will see black boulders lying scattered like lumps of coal. It is said they were formed by the thunderbolts Zeus cast to punish Asopus for raising his hand against his lord.

Having dealt with Aegina's father, Zeus carried the lovely girl away to an island in the Saronic gulf, and there he made her his wife. From this union Aeacus was born.

He grew up to become king of the island, which has been called Aegina ever since.

Though the gods do not as a rule pay heed to the requests of mortals, they made an exception for Aeacus, son of Zeus, for the world had never known a man as god-fearing as he.

Once, tired of the endless wars and quarrels that went on among the petty kingdoms of those days, they sent a terrible drought which ravaged the whole of Greece. Spring came, but not a blade of grass was to be seen in all the land. As was the custom in times of crisis, the starving people went to the oracle at Delphi to learn how this punishment sent by the gods might be lifted from them. The oracle's advice was this:

"Ask Aeacus to beg forgiveness for you."

Soon, Aegina was besieged with messengers from every part of Greece, all bearing the same plea. When Aeacus had heard them, he climbed the island's highest peak, where he sacrificed to Zeus and begged him to take pity on the Greeks before they perished to a man.

His wish was granted on the spot. Heavy black clouds darkened the sky and fruitful rain began to fall upon the thirsty earth. The punishment sent by the gods had ended.

Aeacus was also famous for his love of truth and justice. Such was men's faith in the fairness of his judgement that they would come to Aegina from all over the country to have him settle differences between families and neighbours. And is it surprising that mortals came, when even the gods asked him to resolve their quarrels?

At the great athletic contests, too, Aeacus was always to be found, ready to give the final word whenever a dispute arose. Such was the people's love for him, indeed, that many went to the games merely to catch a glimpse of Aeacus, the most just and truthful man that ever lived.

Even when he died, Aeacus did not cease to judge the deeds of men. As a tribute to his upright character, Pluto entrusted him with the keys of Hades and appointed him as judge in the kingdom of the underworld where, together with Minos and Rhadamanthys, he rewarded or punished the dead according to the deeds they had performed on earth.

Aeacus married Endeis of Megara and by her had two sons: Peleus, who became the father of Achilles, and Telamon, who fathered Ajax, the second greatest hero of the Trojan war after Achilles.

Aeacus was not only just but strong. When Apollo and Poseidon were raising the walls of Troy, at the command of Zeus, they called on Aeacus to help them, believing that thus the walls would be made truly impregnable. In fact, this had the opposite result. When the walls had been completed, three snakes tried to slither up and get into the city. Two of them tried to climb the part built by the gods, but fell and were killed before they reached the top. The third, however, chose the section Aeacus had made. It scaled the wall and wormed its way into the city with a terrifying hiss. Then Apollo prophesied that the city would twice be taken by the Greeks and that on both occasions descendants of Aeacus would be among them. His words proved true; for the first time Troy fell to Heracles, Aeacus' son Telamon was the first to breach its walls, while the second time his grandson Ajax was among the force that stormed it.

Aeacus ruled Aegina with wisdom and with love. The farmers worked hard and reaped bountiful harvests in return for their labour, and the people of the island had never known such years of plenty and happiness. But something

always comes to ruin men's good works – and if no envious mortal can be blamed, it will be a higher, and more
ruthless power. This time it was the goddess Hera, who
hated Aeacus because her husband Zeus had got him by
another woman. When she saw he had become the best-
loved, most respected man on earth, she determined to exact
a hideous revenge.

A single water-snake was all she sent at first. What harm
could one poor water-snake do to an isle the size of Aegina?
And yet the harm was there, just waiting to be hatched; for
the serpent laid thousands upon thousands of eggs and soon
the whole island was swarming with snakes, which pol-
luted every stream and spring the people drank from. Before long they were parched with thirst. Then followed fam-
ine, for the snakes ate every blade of green upon the land.
Stocks of food ran low and not a drop of water could be
found. The people wetted their dry throats with the last of
the wine but when that, too, was gone the situation became hopeless. As if these trials were not enough, Hera
then sent a hot wind from the south, laden with sickness,
and with this final blow the disaster was complete. Starva-
tion, thirst and plague struck down the inhabitants of

Aegina. Pale skeletons that had once been men staggered to the altars leading emaciated beasts, in the faint hope that in offering them they would finally make the gods take pity – but before they could even make the sacrifice they would drop dead from exhaustion. Eventually, there was not a living soul on Aegina but Aeacus and his family. For the first time, his prayers had gone unanswered by the gods – for Hera had succeeded in keeping them all a long way from the island.

Yet in the end Aeacus found a way to make Zeus hear his plea. On Aegina there was a sacred oak which had grown from an acorn off the great tree at Dodona where Zeus was worshipped. Aeacus went and stood beneath it, calling upon the lord of gods and men for help. The moment he did so, a streak of lightning flashed through the cloudless sky, a sign that the god who wields the thunderbolts had heard his cry. In the sudden brightness, Aeacus noticed a long line of ants, busily going to and from their nest within the tree trunk. He stood and watched them for a moment, then raised his arms towards the leafy branches and cried:

"O father Zeus – I know it was you who saved my fam-

*...Aeacus noticed a long line of ants, busily going to and
from their nest within the tree trunk...*

ily and me from death; and by your sign you have shown that you will protect us from here on. But what is life to us if there are no men left to work the earth and make it bear fruit? If I am your son, and you care for me as I believe, do what I beg you now: make these ants men, good-hearted and strong workers who will bring the joy of life to Aegina once more."

When Aeacus' prayer was done, the branches of the oak tree trembled and a rustling in its leaves, which no wind could explain, filled his heart with hope. But by now he was too exhausted to stand and sank down at its roots. Soon sleep overcame him, and while he slept he had a dream. In it he saw the ants' nest once again, with countless streams of the little insects emerging and immediately turning into people. Men, women and children were fanning out in all directions and filling the empty land, while Aeacus walked among them, gazing in their faces, embracing them and kissing them and wishing it would never end. But then he woke; the happy vision faded from before his eyes and pain and sadness clouded his face once more. His glance fell on the ants' nest, but now it was deserted and not a single ant was to be seen. Black despair was welling up in

Aeacus' heart when Telamon came running towards him, shouting breathlessly:

"Father, get up! Something incredible has happened!"

Aeacus rose to his feet. And what did he see? Aegina was filled with people! Men and women were tilling the soil, masons and carpenters were building houses, graceful young girls were carrying water from the springs and little children playing happily, without a care in the world. It was all as if nothing had ever happened to the island. Among the faces that he saw were many that Aeacus remembered from his dream. Everything had come to pass exactly as he had begged Zeus. A new race now peopled Aegina, the Myrmidons, who took their names from the Greek word for the ants they had once been. From these men and women would be born the fearless comrades of Achilles, the splendid Myrmidons who won undying glory in the Trojan war.

Aeacus had a third son after Peleus and Telamon. His name was Phocus and, being the youngest, he was his father's favourite, which aroused the jealousy of his brothers. To make matters worse, as the boy grew he began to surpass them both in speed and strength. Whereas Telamon and Peleus had always defeated the other contestants in the games, now, with the exception of wrestling, where Peleus still reigned supreme, it was Phocus who carried off the victor's laurels. What had once been mere envy on his brothers' part swelled slowly into hatred.

One day, the three brothers were in the stadium when a discus thrown by Telamon flew off course and struck Phocus on the head, killing him instantly. Both Telamon and Peleus were horror-stricken, not only by the gross carelessness which had caused his death, but by the fear that they would be accused of doing it on purpose, for all knew how bitterly the pair of them had hated Phocus. So they decided to bury him secretly. This was the worst course of action they could have taken, and it was made worse still when they were caught red-handed. Exactly what the brothers had feared then followed: they were accused of wilful murder. Their father did not share in this belief, but still advised them to leave Aegina with all speed. This indeed seemed the best solution, so Telamon went to Salamis, while Peleus took refuge in the city of Phthia in Thessaly.

On Salamis, all went well for Telamon. Thanks to his ability he became the ruler of that island, while his courage earned him a place fighting at the side of Heracles in the assault on Troy.

Peleus and his troubled story

When Peleus reached Phthia, he received a warm and sympathetic welcome from king Eurytion, who came to feel such affection and respect for the young man that he gave him a third of his kingdom and the hand of his daughter Antigone in marriage. But in the great hunt for the Calydonian boar, another terrible accident darkened Peleus' life – by sheer mischance he killed Eurytion! At this second harsh blow of fate, Peleus sank into despair. He had taken the life of the man who was at once his benefactor and the father of his wife. There was no question now of his accepting the throne of Phthia when his hands were stained with Eurytion's blood, so he gave up all claim to the kingdom, left his wife in the care of her mother and took up the life of a homeless wanderer. Fate guided his steps to neighbouring Iolcus, where, quite by chance, he met its king, Acastus. Although the hardships of his lonely wanderings had left Peleus looking more like a beggar than a king, Acastus soon realized that this was no ordinary stranger. Indeed, when he looked at him more closely, he saw such noble anguish written in his face that he could not refrain from asking:

"Who are you, stranger, and what troubles you? For here in Iolcus we never leave a traveller without food and shelter; and should he need other help from us we are always willing to oblige."

When Acastus heard that this was Peleus, son of Aeacus, and learned what lay so heavily upon his conscience, he welcomed him with honours and invited him to the palace as his guest. He absolved the young man of all guilt in the killing of Eurytion and helped him, like a father, to throw off the grief that weighed upon his heart.

Then, just when Peleus seemed well on the road to recovery and had found the courage to face his wife once more, a new blow fell: queen Astydameia, the wife of Acastus, fell passionately in love with him. One day, when her husband was away, she told the young man openly of her feelings and finally added:

"I offer you my love, my beauty and my wealth – and when Acastus dies, you shall have the whole of this great

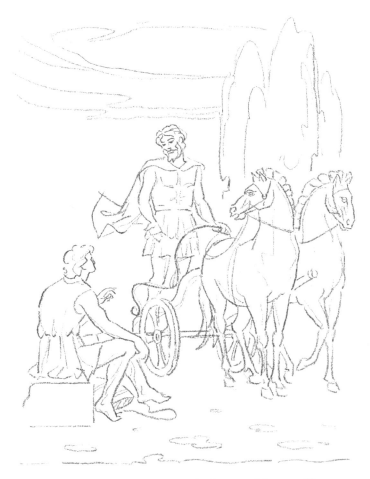

..."Who are you, stranger, and what troubles you?"...

kingdom, too."

But Peleus' answer was very different from the one she had expected.

"I love my wife and respect your husband. He has been my friend and helper. Do not ask of me what I cannot give you."

Astydameia was humiliated by this answer; but instead of being overcome by shame, she took an even wickeder step and sent Peleus' wife Antigone the following letter:

"Since I love you dearly, I must inform you of your husband's intentions. Instead of coming back to you, he plans to marry my daughter."

When Antigone received this message, it was as if the sun had set for ever on her life. Not only had she lost her father, but now her husband was all set to betray her. This cruel stroke of fortune was more than she could bear. Unable to imagine that Astydameia's words might be a lie, the luckless woman took a rope and hanged herself.

Without the slightest qualm of conscience at the appalling consequences of her action, the evil queen thought only of how she might exploit Antigone's death to make Peleus her own – for the young man naturally had no idea why his wife had taken her own life. But she soon saw that he was so torn with grief that a renewed attempt on his honour would be unwise at this stage.

"It can wait," she told herself.

The struggle with Atalanda

Time passed, and the season was approaching when the games in memory of king Pelias were once more to be held. Athletes would come from all over Greece to compete for the victor's laurels in the various events. Among them was a girl, Atalanta, reputed to run faster than the wind. Nobody guessed that she was equally skilled in wrestling; and besides, this was a contest women never took part in.

The finest wrestler in all of Greece was Peleus. So formidable was his reputation that when he announced he would be taking part the other contestants all withdrew, and there was no one left to challenge him.

"Then I shall fight Peleus!" cried Atalanta.

Everyone was taken by surprise.

"How can we allow such a thing! A woman wrestling

with a man? It's unheard of!" protested one of the judges.

"What else can we do?" replied another. "There's not a single man who wants to take him on – and besides, we know both the contestants well, and can be more than sure that they will show absolute respect for the rules and do nothing that might defile these sacred games."

"I agree with you," added a third. "They should be allowed to fight." Finally, all the judges gave their consent. The wrestling match was held – and ended in a draw.

While the two wrestlers held the spectators spellbound with their display of skill and strength, another scene was being enacted nearby, which none of those present could have had the least suspicion of.

Hidden behind some trees, queen Astydameia was following the contest move by move. Seeing Peleus wrestling with a woman, especially one as brave and formidable as Atalanta, her heart beat faster still and faster. Perhaps spurred on by jealousy, perhaps out of simple admiration, her old passion for the hero, which had never died, now flared up again and raced uncontrollably through her veins.

"I must act fast," she told herself, "before Atalanta takes

him from me. His wife is long since dead, and now it's either me or her."

But the thought of taking Peleus for a lover had not crossed Atalanta's mind for an instant, and neither had he set his heart on her; so when Astydameia renewed her offer of love, Peleus turned on the queen in fury.

"The dictates of your conscience are your own affair," he cried, "but you do not have the right to drag down others to your level. Above all, you do not have the right to ask me – and for a second time – to betray the king who gave me shelter and his friendship!"

Astydameia could grasp none of this. All she knew was that Peleus had rejected her advances once again and insulted her into the bargain. She held her tongue, yet inside she was boiling.

"He will pay for this," she muttered, "more dearly even than the first time!" And then she did what Stheneboea had done before her, and what Phaedra, too, had once done in her turn: she denounced Peleus to her husband, giving a distorted version of what had passed between them.

"Acastus," she told him, "I have to tell you that Peleus has shown his thanks for all your kindness by betraying your confidence in him!"

"What do you mean?" the king asked in bewilderment.

"I mean that he tried to steal your wife from you!"

"Who, you? I cannot believe it!" said Acastus in amazement.

"Yes," replied his shameless wife, "and because it is beyond belief, he must be punished harshly."

"But how?" asked Acastus.

"If Peleus is not put to death, he will think that it was I who begged that he be spared," said Astydameia, "and then he will renew his unwelcome attentions."

"I agree with you entirely," answered Acastus in a troubled voice, "yet I cannot kill a guest, for to do so would bring down the wrath of Zeus upon us – and woe betide this house if we break his rules of hospitality!"

"All I know is that Peleus must die," was Astydameia's cold rejoinder. "It is up to you to find the way."

Peleus, a hunter of savage beasts

So Acastus searched for some means of causing Peleus' death without actually doing the deed himself. In the end, he decided to send him to Mount Pelion to hunt the savage beasts that lurked there.

"If he is guilty, let some wild creature kill him," Acastus decided. "Then his punishment will be the work of the gods, and not my doing." So he called some faithful hunting friends, revealed what was troubling him, then instructed them to take Peleus to the mountain and set him to hunt the most ferocious animals of all, until he met his death.

Peleus, who was a skilled and fearless hunter himself, willingly accepted the invitation and set off for Pelion with Acastus' friends. Yet though he slew large numbers of wild beasts there, he did not receive as much as a scratch. Then, as now, hunters were fond of recounting imaginary exploits, and to make sure his word would not be doubted afterwards, Peleus would always cut off the tongues of the animals that he killed and drop them in a pouch slung at his belt; and that is what he did on this expedition, too. Naturally, the other hunters knew nothing of this; and so they could also boast of deeds of valour, through ones they had never performed, they did something else, it certain would impress their comrade immensely: they gathered up the beasts that Peleus had slain, with the intention of passing them off as their own kills.

"If Peleus comes back alive," said one, "we'll mock him for returning empty-handed. If he gets angry and provokes us, it won't be our fault. And if anything should happen to him when he loses his temper, it won't be we who are to blame!"

"A splendid scheme!" agreed another. "If it works – and it must do – then Acastus will reward us generously."

"He's coming," whispered a third, "and with nothing to show for his pains, either. Now's our chance!" And as soon as the hero was in hailing distance, he called out mockingly:

"No luck today, Peleus? And we took you for a hunter!"

"Not even a rabbit? Too bad, eh?" jeered the first of them. "Just see what we have killed – such monsters, too!"

"Well done," Peleus said ironically. "But can you tell me why the animals you slew have got no tongues? Forgive me if I'm wrong – perhaps they have."

The other hunters stared at him in guilty confusion, then examined the dead animals. Not one of them had a tongue.

"And so what?" retorted one of them defiantly, unwilling to admit that Peleus had called their bluff.

"Only this," the hero answered. "Though dead, these animals call you liars by the evidence of their own mouths." And with these words he drew a whole string of cut-off tongues from the pouch that hung at his side.

The game was up. And soon, instead of picking a quarrel with Peleus, as they had planned, the hunters fell out bitterly amongst themselves, each trying to throw the blame upon the others. If Peleus had not parted them, they would have fallen on each other in dead earnest.

When Acastus heard how the hunt had ended, he was filled with chagrin. Not only had his murderous scheme proved a failure, but his friends had been humiliated, too.

"But they're all incompetent, anyhow," he told himself. "Unless I deal with this affair in person, nothing will ever get done." And so saying he went off to find Peleus.

"Let's go hunting on Pelion again," he told him, "but just the two of us this time."

Peleus was willing enough, and after a walk of several hours, when both of them were tired, they sat down by a spring to get their breath back. After he had drunk, Peleus stretched out for a while; but so weary was he that sleep soon overcame him.

"Exactly what I wanted," smiled Acastus; and taking his companion's knife he hid it beneath some animal droppings that lay nearby.

Now the knife Acastus hid was not only the sole means of protection that Peleus carried, but it was a magic weapon, the work of Hephaestus, and no victim could escape its gleaming blade.

"Without it he is doomed," Acastus gloated, "for if he is found here by those I think will find him, he will never live to tell the tale!" And with these words he went and hid himself, leaving Peleus asleep.

Soon afterwards the hero was awakened by the thud of hoofbeats. He rose to see who could be coming, but what met his eyes was not horses but Centaurs galloping towards him – and their intentions were obviously not friendly. Realising the danger he was in, Peleus reached for his knife, only to find an empty sheath. Then he called out to Acastus, but he, too, was nowhere to be found. Meanwhile the Centaurs were rearing savagely, their sharp-tipped lances poised to throw. Peleus felt the hair rise on his neck. He was unarmed and alone. He knew now he had been betrayed.

"How could Acastus have done this to me?" he wondered. "No matter how, I'll go down fighting!" And picking up stones and broken branches, he hurled them at the Centaurs.

But the odds were all against him. The savage creatures only had to get a little closer and they would certainly be able to pierce him with their lances. Then suddenly yet another Centaur burst out from behind a bush. Peleus knew now that his seconds were numbered.

But this Centaur, instead of launching himself on the defenceless hero, wheeled round on his brothers and raising high his arms cried out:

"Can't you stop killing innocent victims?"

"Innocent, you say? He has defiled our spring, and he must die!"

"He has done you no harm – and besides, he is unarmed."

"If he is unarmed, so much the better for us. And if he hasn't harmed us yet, he will do if we let him live. Get out of our way, and make it fast, for this time we are not going to listen to you."

Peleus stared at the Centaur who had defended him. His hair and beard were white, his manner serious and his eyes deep and thoughtful. It could be none other than Cheiron, the wise Centaur whose intelligence and wisdom surpassed that of the gods themselves. And because Cheiron had visionary powers as well, it was not long before his eye divined what lay beneath the animal droppings. Scraping them aside with his hoof, he laid bare the knife. Bending swiftly, he tossed it to Peleus, shouting:

"And now be on your guard! The knife I gave him is a magic one, and nobody escapes its thrust."

Peleus' hand reached up and seized the knife as it flew through the air towards him. As his fingers closed around it his face darkened and grew terrible to behold. The Centaurs halted their advance and looked at him with hesitation in their eyes. The hero drew back his arm and raised it high, ready to charge.

"Get back, I tell you, or you are undone!" cried Cheiron.

At his shout the Centaurs swung round and galloped off into the trees – not so much because they were afraid but more because they did not dare to go against the wishes of their wise old brother Cheiron.

A moment later, Acastus appeared.

"Traitor!" roared Peleus, raising his knife threateningly

again.

"Which of us is a traitor the gods know all too well!" retorted Acastus; and he, too, drew his knife in fury.

"You are neither of you traitors!" shouted Cheiron. "It is Astydameia who has betrayed you both." And the great seer told them the whole story.

"Poor Antigone!" cried Peleus and Acastus together, and fell into each other's arms.

"Astydameia will pay dearly for this," added Acastus.

"Indeed she must pay," said Cheiron.

So Astydameia was tried and condemned to death. The two friends took pity on her and spared her life, but, pursued by those spirits of revenge, the Furies, she lost her mind and died deserted and alone.

The wedding of Peleus and Thetis

Peleus later returned to Phthia and took up his throne once more, but the chief interest in his story from here on lies in his second marriage. For Peleus' next wife was a goddess, a rare honour for a mortal man. It was not unusual for the gods to take ordinary women, but never did a goddess accept a common earth-bound male.

How Peleus became an exception to this rule is a tale in itself.

The goddess who married Peleus was Thetis, the fairest of the Nereids, the lovely daughters of old Nereus, who lived beneath the deep blue waters of the sea. Thetis did not wed Peleus of her own free will, however, but by the ruling of the gods of Olympus; and the gods did not make their decision without good reason.

The beautiful goddess of the sea was beloved of Zeus himself, who had long wanted to make her his wife. Thetis, though, would not agree to such a marriage; not because she found Zeus unattractive – quite the opposite – but because she did not wish to embitter her good friend Hera.

Nevertheless, Zeus persisted in his attentions. What he did not know, however, was that it was written by the Fates that when Thetis married, she would bear a son who would grow to be more powerful than his father. This was a secret known only to the titan Prometheus, who also knew that if Zeus married Thetis, the son she bore would cast him from his throne. Prometheus had long kept his knowledge from Zeus' ears because the latter had chained him to a rock in the mountains of the Caucasus. At last, however, the titan decided to reveal his secret, and then the ruler of the world realized how such a marriage was to be feared.

"But Thetis must not marry any other god, either," thought Zeus. "Only a mortal can become her husband, and then her son, however strong he grows to be, will pose no threat to the throne of Olympus; for he, too, will only be a mortal."

Thetis was grieved beyond all words when she heard of Zeus' decision; but the goddess Hera, who had not forgotten how considerately Nereus' daughter had behaved towards her, came to offer sympathy and encouragement.

"I know the proper husband for a goddess is a god and not a man," she told her; "but the decrees of Zeus cannot be altered, whether they be for good or ill. There is, however, a mortal who is equal to the gods in all respects, a man of sufficient worth for you to take him as your husband."

How could poor Thetis say that he was equal to the gods in all respects but one: that while she had the gift of eternal youth, her mortal husband would grow old and die. How could such a union hold any appeal for her when she knew that the kinder and more noble her husband was, the greater would her suffering be when his life reached its end? What had she done to deserve such a fate, when she could, had she wished, have married Zeus himself and been by now the first among the goddesses!

"It grieves me deeply to see you so sorrowful and filled with doubts," Hera went on, "but there is a man I would like you to consider, a hero and a noble king who is respected and loved by gods and men alike. His name is Peleus, son of Aeacus – and Aeacus, in turn, was son of Zeus. And know this, too: it is written by the Fates that you will bear him a son who is destined to become the greatest war-leader in all Greece!"

"And then I shall weep not only for the loss of my husband, but for my poor son's death, as well," retorted Thetis. "Could any woman know a harsher fate?"

"I understand your feelings," replied Hera tenderly, "but I tell you once again – Zeus has decided this."

"Then hear what I have decided," Thetis flared. "I shall not marry Peleus unless he can wrestle me into submission!"

Hera knew exactly what this meant, and left in disappointment. For she was aware that if anyone could defeat both deity and mortal in wrestling, it was Thetis. She returned to Olympus with a gloomy face to report the sea goddess's defiant stand to the council of the gods.

They were all taken by surprise, certain that in such a contest Thetis would defeat Peleus and that thus, despite Zeus' wishes, their wedding would never take place. Only Aphrodite did not share their gloom.

"There is another kind of strength might prove triumphant in a contest such as this," she smiled, "– the strength of love!"

Zeus understood. And so the council of the gods finally accepted Thetis' terms. Then they appointed Cheiron to break the news to Peleus, who, unlike the sea god's daughter, was delighted at the prospect. As for wrestling with her, he said to Cheiron:

"I shall defeat her, even if she wrestles better than Atalanta. I shall fight with every last ounce of my strength if that is the only way I can win her for my own."

"She may not be a better wrestler than Atalanta," replied Cheiron, "but she has powers your first opponent certainly did not have. Like her father, old Nereus, Thetis can suddenly change her shape while fighting and become a lion, a snake, a bull or even water, and that is where you will face your greatest difficulty."

But Peleus made light of this and was determined to go ahead, confident that he would win, whatever form his lovely opponent took.

"Then all that remains is for me to tell you where she can be found," concluded Cheiron. "You must go to Cape Sepias, at the southernmost tip of Pelion. A shrine dedicated to Thetis stands there and the goddess comes out on the shore at each full moon. What follows is in your hands."

At the next full moon, Peleus went to the beach and waited anxiously, hidden behind a bush. Then, suddenly, there was a swirl of dark waters and Thetis appeared. Tall, fair and blue-eyed, she dazzled Peleus with her beauty. No vision or dream could have been lovelier than the figure which now stood before him. At the very thought that this divine creature might become his wife, a shudder of delight ran through the hero's body.

"I shall defeat her," he resolved, "or die." And without a moment's hesitation he flung himself upon the goddess and seized her by the waist. Thetis let out a cry of surprise

*...without a moment's hesitation Peleus flung himself
upon the goddess and seized her by the waist...*

and fear, but she soon realized who her opponent was and turned on him in fury. She fought back savagely, but Peleus would not release his hold; she struggled to get free, but he held her in an iron grip; she tried to throw him off balance – and again her efforts were in vain. Seeing what a formidable wrestler had her in his grasp, she realized that only by using all the means at her disposal could she wrest the victory from him. "Now he will see!" she gasped, and in a trice she transformed herself into a spray of water and soaked him to the skin. Then she became a whirlwind and blew Peleus off his feet, and then a lion, drawing bloody claw-marks down his body, and then a horse-fly which stung him without mercy, and then a snake which wound its coils around his struggling limbs. But the harder she attacked, the more furiously Peleus fought back, determined to win her for his own however high the cost. Finally Thetis turned herself into a giant squid, and when Peleus seized her she squirted him from head to foot with sooty ink. Yet still the hero did not give up hope and kept his hold with grim determination. Nothing would make him give the struggle up, the goddess saw. Whatever shape she took, he clung as fiercely as before. So impressed was Thetis by his courage that she abandoned her disguises and became once more the lovely goddess who had risen from the waves. Peleus immediately clasped her in his arms for fear of losing her, but by now she had lost all will to escape. Looking at the hero tenderly, the lovely maiden melted into his embrace. Thetis had given up the fight, and Peleus had won his sea goddess. Thanks to the power of love, the impossible had been achieved. Aphrodite had been right.

Their wedding took place soon afterwards; and it was at the splendid marriage-feast of Peleus and Thetis, attended by all the gods and goddesses, that the jealous Eris let the fateful golden apple fall. It bore the inscription: "to the fairest" – only three words, but ones which brought disaster on mankind.

That fascinating story, however, comes as the prologue to another book: 'The Trojan War'. It is enough to say here that as Prometheus had foretold, Thetis gave birth to a son who grew up to be mightier than his father: Achilles, the greatest general who ever led the Greeks into battle.

THE HUNTING
OF THE CALYDONIAN BOAR

Atalanta and Meleager

King Iasion of Arcadia was about to become a father, and it was his dearest wish that his wife should bear him a son to succeed him on the throne. But instead of a baby boy, she gave birth to a daughter, and this enraged the king so much that he ordered his servants to take the new-born child and leave it in the mountains. Neither his wife's tears nor his parents' pleas would move the cruel king, and so the unlucky infant was taken far away and abandoned in a forest, near Calydon. There, however, she was found by a bear, who took pity on her, gave her its milk and reared her with its cubs. And so the little girl was saved from death until at last some hunters stumbled across her. They took her with them, gave her the name of Atalanta and raised her as their own. Growing up in the forest with the huntsmen and following them in their daily search for food, the little girl led such a healthy and active life that in the end she could bound up hillsides with all the agility of a mountain goat and race through the forest clearings with the fleetness of a deer.

She grew to be a huntress of such skill that only the goddess Artemis could match her in the chase. And so it was not long before the name of Atalanta was well-known throughout Greece. Although in those days athletic competitions were not open to women, an exception was made in her case; she took part in the games with the young men, and always defeated them in both archery and running. In wrestling, too, she was unbeatable, putting all the other wrestlers to shame when she alone had the courage to take on Peleus, the most formidable fighter of them all. When a contest ended, and the moment came for her to mount the stand and have the victor's laurels placed upon her brow, the crowds would cheer so loudly that one would have thought that she was no mere winner in some game of skill or speed, but a great and mighty goddess descended from Olympus.

Her talents and her peerless beauty made every bold young man in Greece desire her for his wife. But Atalanta loved the free life of the mountains and had no wish to be married. Whenever a hero sought her hand, she would give him this reply:

"If you want me for a wife, you must outrun me." And since there was no man in the world to match her fleetness, Atalanta continued to live the life that suited her, breathing the free, cold air of the wild hillsides.

Among the men who loved her was the hero Meleager, but for fear of being humbled he never showed his love. Superb athlete though he was, he knew he would meet defeat if he challenged Atalanta to run against him. And so he buried his feelings and later married Cleopatra, the daughter of king Idas. Yet he never forgot Atalanta, and this became clear in the famous hunt for the Calydonian boar.

Meleager was the son of king Oeneus of Calydon, and when he was only seven days old the Fates came to his mother, Althaea, and warned her that her son would die the moment that the log which now lay smouldering in her hearth had burned to ash. When she heard these words, Althaea seized a pitcher of water and doused the fire, then took the blackened lump of wood and hid it at the bottom of a chest.

The famous hunt

Meleager lived, and grew into a strong and handsome young man, a mighty hero and an invincible warrior, unmatched by any of his generation. Neither spear nor sword nor arrow could harm him, and no disease or danger was able to strike him down; for death could not touch him till fire consumed the log which his mother had hidden so carefully away.

Meleager's father, Oeneus, was so proud of his son that

every year he made rich sacrifices to all the gods to thank them for giving him not only power and wealth but a son who was a worthy heir to the throne of Calydon. One year, however, he made a fatal omission: he offered gifts to all the gods but Artemis. The sun god Helios, who sees all from his vantage-point in the heavens, was well aware of what Oeneus had failed to do; and since he had given his word to Artemis that he would report any lack of respect that any mortal showed her, Oeneus' blunder soon reached the goddess's ears. The punishment which then fell on Calydon was terrible. A huge wild boar with tusks like giant needles began to uproot all the land, ravaging the crops, knocking down the shepherds' huts and killing men and animals alike, while those foolhardy enough to imagine they could hunt it down soon met their death in the unequal struggle.

Seeing how difficult it was going to be to rid his country of this scourge, Oeneus decided to organise a great hunting party, in which many heroes would take part. First and foremost among them, of course, would be his own son, Meleager.

From every corner of Greece the boldest and the bravest came in answer to Oeneus' call. Among them were Castor and Polydeuces from Sparta, Peleus and Eurytion from Phthia, Telamon from Salamis, Idas from Messene, Theseus from Athens, Peirithous from Larissa, Jason from Iolcus, Admetus from Pherae, Amphiaraus from Argos, Ancaeus and Cepheus from Tegea – and last, but not least, Atalanta.

Now while all the male huntsmen were welcomed by their comrades, there were objections to Atalanta. Ancaeus and Cepheus began to protest.

"Why do we need a woman in the hunt?" asked Ancaeus.

"She'll only bring us bad luck," added his brother Cepheus.

But Meleager defended Atalanta stoutly:

"There's not a better hunter among us!" he shouted.

Cepheus knew he was right, and held his tongue; but Ancaeus retorted:

"We'll soon see who is best when we come to the chase!"

"You speak more wisely than you know," agreed Meleager; and in the end, they all consented to let Atalanta accompany them.

Oeneus entertained the huntsmen royally for nine days,

and on the tenth day they set out, each of them eager to kill the wild boar for himself and thus win not only the monster's pelt and tusks but lasting honour and glory.

The chase began. The dogs streamed out ahead, sniffing at the earth and barking furiously to flush the creature from its lair.

However, two Centaurs who happened to be nearby were drawn by the noise and when they saw Atalanta close behind the hounds and all alone, they were so inflamed by her beauty that they came galloping up to ravish her. A fierce struggle then broke out between the lone maiden and the lustful Centaurs, who had never for a moment imagined that her lovely body could conceal such power. Meleager, who was not far behind, ran to Atalanta's aid when he saw she was in danger; but he soon realized that she needed no help from him or any of the other heroes who came running in support. The two Centaurs were already lying dead. All who saw them were filled with admiration for the girl and realized how unjust Ancaeus had been in trying to exclude her from the hunt.

Soon afterwards, the dogs tracked down the boar. Meleager and Atalanta were far out on the other flank when

it suddenly charged into the hunters and fell on all those
who happened to lie in its path. Within seconds two brave
heroes lay dead and two more gravely wounded, gored by
the giant tusks of a monster twice the size of any normal
boar. The hunters stood appalled. If this first brief encounter had wreaked such havoc in their ranks, what more lay
in store for them? But Jason, Theseus and Telamon plucked
up their courage and began to hurl lances and shoot arrows
at the beast. In vain, however, for it lunged in all directions
with the speed of lightning, preventing them from taking

careful aim. One of Telamon's arrows grazed its back, to be sure, but this caused no injury; and the shaft loosed by Peleus a second later glanced off one of the boar's tusks, struck Eurytion in the chest and killed him instead. This third death among their numbers discouraged the hunters still more, and they began to fear that the boar was protected by some divine power – perhaps by Artemis herself. Not only was it invulnerable, but the disrespect they showed in hunting it was costing them the blood of their comrades.

This was where matters stood when Atalanta and Meleager came running up. One bowshot from the huntress and the whole situation changed. Her arrow thudded into the wild boar's head, just below the ear. The beast let out a great squeal of agony, and though it managed to stay upright, its moments were now numbered.

Most of the heroes greeted Atalanta's success with enthusiastic cries, except for Ancaeus who sneered:

"Do you call that a shot? See what a man can do!" And with these words he lifted his battle-axe and brought it down with terrifying strength; but the monster swerved aside from the falling blade, and the next instant Ancaeus lay cut between the legs by his own stroke – and a man no longer.

Letting out shrill howls of pain, the boar was meanwhile running round in circles, trying to dislodge Atalanta's arrow from its head with scrabbling hooves but only succeeding in enlarging the wound and bringing forth torrents of blood. A few moments later, the hunters got in a second successful shot: taking skilful aim, Amphiaraus took out one of its eyes. The monster bellowed in agony and sought desperately for some way of escape. But now Theseus was standing in its path. Gathering what strength was left to it, redoubled by the fear of death, the boar charged straight down on the hero. Too late, however, for Meleager sprang in from one side and quick as lightning plunged his keen sword through its flanks, right into the heart. It was all over now. The fearsome creature sank dead to the ground. The hunt for the Calydonian boar had ended.

The sad fate of Meleager

Unfortunately, the same could not be said for the goddess's vengeful anger. Artemis could not bear to see the scourge lifted from Calydon when its people had treated her with such scant respect. By neglecting to offer up sacrifice, they had treated her as if she were some minor deity. As luck would have it, the opportunity to salve her wounded pride came when Meleager skinned the boar and offered the pelt to Atalanta.

"Your arrow struck home first," he said. "The prize belongs to you." Hearing these words, Plexippus, Meleager's uncle on his mother's side, sprang up, deeply offended.

"What right have you to give the prize to Atalanta?" he

demanded. "You killed the boar; and if you do not want its hide then I should have it – for I am senior in rank here."

"The honour goes to Atalanta," Meleager replied. "For if she had not wounded the boar I might never have been able to kill it. Besides, it would have died from the wound she inflicted whether I had dealt the final blow or not – and that's the truth."

"The truth is that your head's been turned by a woman," sneered Plexippus' brother, glaring at the young man in hatred.

This was more than Meleager could tolerate. Blinded by fury to the fact that these men were his mother's brothers, he drew his sword and, his hand guided by the invisible Artemis, he killed them both.

Like his mother, Meleager's two uncles were from Pleuron, a city inhabited by the Curetes, a race of savage warriors; and when news of the murder reached their ears they declared war on the people of Calydon. Artemis had achieved her purpose.

"Calydon will be burned to the ground," she gloated.

However, with Meleager as their leader, the Calydonians not only withstood the assault of the Curetes but chased them back to their stronghold at Pleuron, where they were forced to take refuge. While all Calydon regarded the young man as its saviour, there was one among them who longed for his downfall – and this was none other than his own mother. Althaea could not bring herself to believe that the boy she had borne in her own womb and had loved so deeply could have killed two of her brothers and then gone on to humiliate what was left of her family – for her other two brothers were by now trapped like rats in their castle at Pleuron. All Althaea's motherly instincts curdled into hate, and she prayed day and night to Pluto and Persephone, the rulers of Hades, to take her son down into their dark kingdom.

When Meleager heard of this, he was so deeply hurt that he abandoned his pursuit of the Curetes instantly and shut himself up in his house with his wife Cleopatra, an embittered man. Never in his wildest imagination could he have dreamed that his own mother would desire his death.

Without a leader, the fortunes of the Calydonians took a turn for the worse. The Curetes broke the siege of Pleuron and came out in pursuit of their tormentors, sowing death and destruction in their path. In vain did his fellow-citizens beg Meleager to return to battle and save Calydon.

He was deaf to his father's commands, unyielding to his wife's pleas and his sister's supplications. Even his mother, seeing the awful fate which threatened the city, now repented her harsh words and begged him to take up arms and drive the enemy back before it was too late. Meleager, however, was so offended that he stubbornly ignored them all, while the Curetes in the meantime broke down the city gates and entered Calydon, where they burned, slaughtered and plundered in vengeful frenzy. They reached the very doors of Meleager's house, determined to tear it down, but still he did not move, so great was his anger and his stubbornness! In the end, his young wife Cleopatra fell at his feet and tearfully begged him to save Calydon while there was still time, and to pity its women and children, who would be led away into slavery. And then she added:

"But perhaps you would prefer to see your own wife and sister dragged off and dishonoured!"

These words finally broke the hero's resolve. He sprang up, buckled on his shining armour, seized his weapons and lunged into the fray. The mere sight of him was enough to sow panic among the Curetes, who ran helter-skelter to escape his deadly arrows. But many were not quick enough and fell lifeless to the ground. In a matter of hours Calydon was freed of its invaders, who fled back to Pleuron to take refuge in their fortress. However, among those Meleager had killed in the fighting were his remaining two uncles, and that was the worst thing he could have done. As soon as Althaea learned that her son had robbed her of the last of her brothers, her old hatred was rekindled and she once more begged the gods for vengeance.

"If no mortal can kill him, then you can!" she cried. And so long and loud were her complaints that in the end the Fates appeared before her.

"You call upon the gods in vain," they said. "They can do nothing until you take the log you once drew burning from the fire and cast it back into the flames."

The moment she heard these words, Althaea ran, filled with hatred for her murdering son, opened the trunk where the blackened lump of wood had lain for all these years, and hurled it back into the fire.

At that very instant, Apollo flew down from Olympus

and ran to join the battle where Meleager was pursuing the
Curetes; and as the log was crumbling into ash, he lifted
his deadly bow and took the hero's life.

Robbed by the gods of what no mortal could have taken,
he descended, racked with bitterness and pain, to the dark
kingdom of the shadows. And so ends the story of Meleager, a tale so sad that when Heracles heard it, his eyes are
said to have filled with tears.

Atalanta and Melanion

As for Atalanta, the fame she won in hunting down the
Calydonian boar at last persuaded her father to accept her
as his daughter. Indeed, such was his paternal concern now
that he even decided to find her a husband.

Atalanta's hand in marriage was sought by Melanion,
who had also taken part in the boar hunt, but the proud
maiden did not even want to hear of losing her freedom.
Seeking some means of escape, she told her father:

"I shall run a race with him. Melanion can set off before
me. If he finishes first, I will marry him – but if I overtake
him on the way, I will kill him instead."

For all Atalanta's confidence that her suitor would never dare accept a challenge such as this, Melanion was so much in love with her that he decided to take the risk.

Fortunately Aphrodite, who always helps true lovers, came to the young man's aid. She gave him three golden apples, with instructions to drop them in Atalanta's path whenever he saw her drawing close.

Melanion did exactly what the goddess told him. When Atalanta began to catch him up, he tossed the first of the apples over his shoulder. So richly did the ball of burnished gold gleam in the sunlight that Atalanta could not resist its beauty, and stooped to pick it up. Later in the race, he let a second apple fall, and later still a third; and so Melanion crossed the winning line ahead.

The hero was delighted with his victory; and Atalanta, who wished him no ill, opened her arms and received him as her husband.

The two young people were married at once, but they did not enjoy their love for long. They were punished by Zeus because they spent their wedding night in the garden of his temple. So offended was he that he transformed them into two stone lions who stood looking mournfully into each other's eyes, forever frozen in time, unable to exchange a tender word or an embrace. And there they remained, an object of pity to passers-by – that pity which seems rare among the gods and springs more readily from human hearts.

INDEX OF NAMES for all volumes

The volume number, ①, ②, ③ to ⑧, precedes the page number or numbers on which the name is mentioned (14-16, 132, 233 etc.).

The more important references are indicated with bold faced type; the ligher print shows other useful references.

GREEK MYTHOLOGY SERIES

* * *

The index of names appearing in this volume
can be also found on our web site:
www.sigmabooks.gr.

The site also includes **mythological maps**
and extensive extracts from all our books.